P9-DMS-027

Who's That in the White House?

The Progressive Years

1901 to 1933

THEODORE
ROOSEVELT

WILLIAM H.
TAFT

WOODROW
WILSON

WARREN G.
HARDING

CALVIN
COOLIDGE

HERBERT C.
HOOVER

by Rose Blue and Corinne J. Naden

RSVP
RAINTREE
STECK-VAUGHN
PUBLISHERS
The Steck-Vaughn Company

Austin, Texas

*To the memory of Mary Lee Graeme and to Rose's mom,
two very gutsy ladies.*

Published by Raintree Steck-Vaughn Publishers, an imprint of Steck-Vaughn Company

Publishing Director: Walter Kossmann
Editor: Shirley Shalit
Consultant: Andrew Frank, University of Florida

Project Manager: Lyda Guz
Electronic Production: Scott Melcer
Photo Editor: Margie Foster

Library of Congress Cataloging-in-Publication Data
Blue, Rose.
The progressive years 1901 to 1933 / by Rose Blue and Corinne J. Naden.
p.   cm. — (Who's that in the White House?)
Includes bibliographical references and index.
Summary: Discusses the lives and political careers of Theodore Roosevelt, William Howard Taft, Woodrow Wilson, Warren Harding, Calvin Coolidge, and Herbert Hoover.
ISBN 0-8172-4303-8
1. Presidents — United States — Biography — Juvenile literature.   2. United States — Politics and government — 1901-1953 — Juvenile literature.   [1. Presidents.   2. United States — Politics and government — 1901-1953.]   I. Naden, Corinne J.   II. Title.
III. Series: Blue, Rose.   Whos that in the White House?
E176.1.B674   1998

973.9'099 — dc21
[B]

97-14710
CIP   AC

Acknowledgments
The authors wish to thank Harold C. Vaughan of Fort Lee, New Jersey,
for his critical reading of the manuscript.
Photography credits: Title page: (all) National Portrait Gallery, The Smithsonian Institution; p. 4 North Carolina Division of Archives & History; p. 6 Courtesy Franklin D. Roosevelt Presidential Library; p. 7 National Portrait Gallery, The Smithsonian Institution; pp. 8, 10 Theodore Roosevelt Collection, Harvard College Library; p. 11 Library of Congress; p. 15 The Granger Collection; p. 17 Brown Brothers; p. 19 The Bettmann Archive; p. 21 The Granger Collection; p. 22 National Portrait Gallery, The Smithsonian Institution; p. 24 The Granger Collection; p. 26 Brown Brothers; p. 27 Library of Congress; pp. 29, 31 The Granger Collection; p. 32 National Portrait Gallery, The Smithsonian Institution; p. 34 Corbis-Bettmann; p. 38 UPI/Corbis-Bettmann; p. 39 The Granger Collection; pp. 41, 42 UPI/Corbis-Bettmann; p. 43 The Granger Collection; p. 44 UPI/Corbis-Bettmann; p. 47 Brown Brothers; p. 50 National Portrait Gallery, The Smithsonian Institution; p. 52 White House Historical Association; p. 55 The Granger Collection; p. 56 Brown Brothers; p. 58 The Granger Collection; p. 60 National Portrait Gallery, The Smithsonian Institution; p. 62 White House Historical Association; p. 63, 65 Culver Pictures; p. 66 Corbis-Bettmann; p. 68 The Granger Collection; p. 69 National Portrait Gallery, The Smithsonian Institution; p. 71 White House Historical Association; p. 72 Culver Pictures; p. 74 (middle) Brown Brothers, (bottom) Culver Pictures; p. 76 UPI/Corbis-Bettmann; p. 77 The Granger Collection; p. 79 Culver Pictures; p. 81 UPI/Corbis-Bettmann.

Cartography: GeoSystems, Inc.

Printed and bound in the United States
1 2 3 4 5 6 7 8 9 0 LB 01 00 99 98 97

Contents

*N*o one word can truly and accurately describe the United States in the period from 1901 until 1933, from Teddy Roosevelt to Herbert Hoover. It was a time of progressive policies, of active government. It was a time of isolation, of a longing for "the good old days." It was a time of change. And much change did take place. Women finally got the vote in 1920 after a long and often discouraging struggle. The Wright Brothers spent a few wobbly moments in the air above Kitty Hawk, North Carolina, in 1903 and forever changed the way folks got around the globe. The Panama Canal, which opened in 1914, changed the way ships got from one ocean to another. Robert E. Peary found the North Pole in 1909 and the country nearly lost San Francisco in

The Wright Brothers at Kitty Hawk, North Carolina, where, on December 17, 1903, the first manned flight of an aircraft powered by a gasoline engine reached a speed of 30 mph and flew 120 feet.

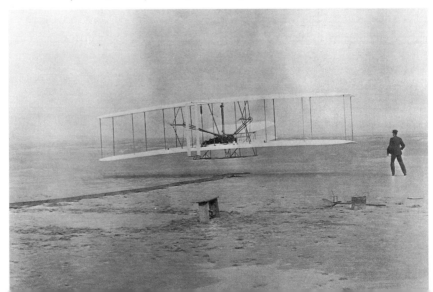

an earthquake in 1906. William Taft's administration saw the number of U.S. states climb to 48, where it would stay until 1959, when a war hero named Eisenhower lived in the White House.

It was a time of progress, but also a time of terrible destruction. The United States tried hard to stay out of the war that erupted in Europe in 1914. But by 1917 it had joined the worldwide conflict. President Woodrow Wilson devoted his life, his administration, and his health to world peace.

It was a strange period—of progress, of war, of peace efforts, of discovery, of inventions, of growing industry, of bigger and better everything. It was a time of more freedom and of more taxes. It was a time of rapidly expanding cities, of poverty, of slums and poor working conditions, and of dishonest politicians who took advantage of everyone. It was also a period of isolation. Stay out of Europe's problems, said some. Let America be, said others. "Keep cool with Coolidge" was the campaign slogan of the 1924 election.

Who knows where the era would have gone had 1929 not ended as it did. Who knows what name it would have been given. However, everything was overshadowed by the unthinkable disaster that struck as the decade of the 1920s came to a close. The mighty economic strength of the brash and splendidly arrogant young nation came tumbling down on its astonished collective head. Stocks became worthless when the New York Stock Exchange crashed on October 29, 1929. Lots of people had most of their money invested in the stock market. With the crash went their hopes and dreams, schemes and deals, power and prestige. The dollars—many and not so many—of millions of Americans were gone. The giddy ride on the roller coaster to wealth was over. So were the lives of many Americans who killed themselves as the only way out of such financial ruin.

The Progressive Years deals with the six men who called the White House home during that 32-year period. They were a varied lot and their influence on the country was varied, too.

These shacks built by unemployed men were photographed in 1933 on an empty lot at West and Charleton Streets in New York City.

Theodore "Teddy" Roosevelt and Wilson get high marks in the performance department. Taft is about average. Coolidge, or "Silent Cal," is known more for saying nothing than doing anything. According to an oft-quoted story, a reporter once said to him: "Mr. President, I made a bet that I could get more than two words out of you." Coolidge replied, "You lose." Hoover promised "two chickens in every pot and a car in every garage." What he got was the stock market crash and an international depression. And poor Warren Harding. He generally hits the bottom of the presidential list, mostly because of his scandal-ridden administration.

Only two of the six Presidents during the progressive years —Roosevelt and Wilson—served two terms. Coolidge took over upon Harding's death and then spent four years in the White House on his own. Taft left after one term to do something he really wanted to do—serve on the Supreme Court. And Hoover left because the country really wanted him out.

The era could be called many things. Progressive is just one of them. It began with the aggressive policies of Teddy Roosevelt and ended as the United States faced the worst economic disaster in its history. These were, indeed, changeable, exciting, anxiety-filled, and progressive years.

Chapter One

T. Roosevelt: Larger than Life

Theodore Roosevelt (1901-1909)

*T*heodore Roosevelt gave his country a new hero, a new breed of politician, tireless energy, and the teddy bear. An avid hunter, he was once pictured in a cartoon sparing the life of a bear cub. After that, toy bears were called teddy bears.

The twenty-sixth President looked a bit like a teddy bear himself. From a spindly, asthmatic youth, he grew into a 200-pound, robust man with a great barrel chest, a droopy mustache, a wide grin, and a rather high-pitched voice. He stood about five feet eight inches tall and was nearly blind in his left eye from a hard blow suffered during a boxing match. He was a scholar, a soldier, a rancher, and an important force in shaping the office of the presidency and expanding its powers. For Theodore Roosevelt, national unity ranked above personal interest, class, or section of the country. He was the keeper of the common good. He involved the United States in European and Asian affairs and won the Nobel Peace Prize in 1906.

Teddy Roosevelt was born into a family of wealth, culture, dedication, and historical connections. His ancestors had emigrated from Holland in 1644. His grandfather was a New York tycoon—a person of exceptional wealth and power—who ranked with the likes of such notable, powerful, and wealthy families as the Astors and the Vanderbilts. His father, Theodore senior, was a merchant. Teddy called him, "the best man I ever knew." His mother, Martha Bulloch, was an aristocrat from Georgia who remained staunchly loyal to the South throughout the Civil War. Martin Van Buren, the eighth U.S. President, was his third cousin, and his fifth cousin was Franklin D. Roosevelt, who would become the nation's thirty-second and longest-serving President.

Theodore Roosevelt is the only President, so far, born in New York City, in the family home on East 20th Street. The date was October 17, 1858. Although his grandmother said he was pretty, his mother thought he looked rather like a turtle. Teddy was the second of four children. His brother, Elliott, would become the father of Eleanor Roosevelt, Franklin's wife and First Lady.

Teddy was a sickly lad who spent a good deal of his early years in bed and had to be tutored at home. This gave him plenty of time to become an avid reader. His asthma, however, did

not keep him from trouble. His father once chased him all around the house because he bit his sister on the arm. By the age of seven he had developed a passionate interest in animals, which he kept all his life, and vowed to become a zoologist.

Perhaps it is just as well that he became involved in politics instead since no zoologist has yet made it to the Oval Office. By the age of 18, he was ready for Harvard. A serious student, he also worked on building up his body, which he did in the college gym. He graduated in 1880, ranking 21 out of a class of 177. That year also, he married Alice Hathaway Lee of a well-known Boston family.

They had one daughter, Alice, born in 1884. She lived to be 96 years old and grew up with her father's spirited personality. She was so outspoken

Teddy Roosevelt took up boxing as a sport during his years at Harvard College.

that she generally upset everybody. Once in office, Roosevelt was to remark: "I can be President of the United States, or I can control Alice. I cannot possibly do both."

As a young husband, he went to Columbia Law School, where he quickly discovered he had no taste at all for the practice of law. He stuck to it for a year but never did take the bar exam. For recreation, he rode horseback in Central Park, climbed mountains, went to New York's fanciest parties, and joined a club of Republican party members. His friends were aghast. They said only the "lowest elements" entered politics.

Perhaps so, but Roosevelt seemed to like it. So, in 1881, at the age of 23 he won a seat in the New York State Assembly. He immediately threw himself into his work, gaining public support for his vote to limit the factory workday for women and children and his pledge to abolish sweatshops. That was the term given to unhealthy, unfair working conditions forced upon many poor and uneducated, often immigrant workers. He also made a few enemies among the older conservative Republicans in Albany with his charge against wealthy financier Jay Gould. Declaring that Gould had tried to bribe a state supreme court judge, Roosevelt called him a member of the "most dangerous of all dangerous classes, the wealthy criminal class." That did not sit well in Albany, the capital of New York State.

Roosevelt left Albany anyway in 1884 when his young wife died two days after Alice's birth. Distraught, he headed west for Dakota Territory, leaving his infant daughter in the family's care. For two years, he became a rancher, branding and herding cattle. Apparently he was good at it for he earned the respect of his ranch hands. He never quite got a handle on ranch talk, however, for he often told his horse to "hasten forward quickly" instead of "giddyap."

TR, as he liked to be called, returned east in 1886 and lost a bid to become mayor of New York City. But fortune smiled that December when he married Edith Kermit Carow of Connecticut,

The Roosevelt family in 1894, including Teddy, Archibald (in his father's arms), Theodore, Alice, Kermit, Edith (Roosevelt's second wife), and Ethel.

whom he had known as a child. They began their long and happy marriage with a ceremony in London at which, for some reason, the groom wore bright orange gloves. Besides Alice, their lively household would eventually include five more children: Theodore, Kermit, Ethel, Archibald, and Quentin. All five served during World War I and/or World War II. Ethel was a nurse with the American Ambulance Hospital in Paris during World War I. Archibald was severely wounded in both wars, and Quentin, the youngest, was shot down over France and killed by German fighters in World War I.

In 1889, President Benjamin Harrison named TR to the U.S. Civil Service Commission, where he served until 1895. Roosevelt moved a job that hardly anyone noticed into the national spotlight. He declared he would clean up the Civil Service system. People would be hired for Civil Service jobs on merit, not political favors. "Let the chips fall where they will," he told admiring reporters.

Teddy's star was on the rise. Woe to any corrupt members of the New York City Police Department when TR was made commissioner in 1895. He fought everybody, Republicans and Democrats alike. He condemned tenements, ordering some of these squalid buildings that usually housed the poor to be torn down. He doubled Civil Service jobs and sometimes patrolled the precincts, or police beats, himself to keep everybody on their toes. He made his biggest headlines, however, by closing down saloons on Sunday to enforce the Sunday Excise Law, which banned the sale of alcohol on that day. Generally speaking, the ordinary man on the street was not too pleased with that action, but TR replied, "I do not deal with public sentiment. I deal with the law." And on he charged.

Roosevelt supported Republican William McKinley—somewhat reluctantly—during the presidential election of 1896. In turn, President McKinley—somewhat reluctantly—named him assistant secretary of the Navy in 1897. With the actual secretary, John Long, in poor health, TR was often running the show and lost no opportunity to make himself heard. He was one of the first to see what airplanes could mean to the military in war and asked a panel to study the "new flying machine" of Samuel P. Langley. He called for annexing Hawaii to stop possible Japanese expansion, and he wanted the United States to attack Spanish-held Cuba. It would be, he said, a "bully war."

TR finally got his war in 1898 after the American battleship *Maine* mysteriously blew up in the harbor of Havana, Cuba, on February 15. He sent a cable to Commodore George Dewey in the Pacific, ordering Dewey to make sure the

Teddy Roosevelt poses with his Rough Riders, heroes of the charge up Kettle Hill, Cuba, June 24, 1898.

Spanish fleet did not leave the Asian coast to come to the aid of Spanish forces in Cuba. TR had absolutely no authority to send the cable, but it led to Dewey's easy victory over Spain at Manila Bay in the Philippines on May 1. By then, the United States had declared war on Spain. TR quickly resigned his post as assistant secretary of the Navy. He rounded up an improbable group of sportsmen, cowboys, and old buddies to form the First Volunteer Cavalry Regiment. Off they went to Cuba with Colonel Theodore Roosevelt in command. On June 24, 1898, TR led his so-called Rough Riders in a charge up Kettle Hill in San Juan (usually reported as the charge up San Juan Hill). According to his commanding officer's report, Roosevelt's leadership was spectacular. Although the actual charge had doubtful importance to the war's outcome, there was little doubt that TR was a courageous man. He came home a war hero.

With "Teddy" now on everyone's lips—he hated that nickname—New York Republicans knew a way to the governor's chair when they saw one. Not Senator Thomas Platt of New York, however. Platt, the big Republican boss in the state, just didn't like Roosevelt. And considering TR's constant attacks on big business and big politics, he had reason. But with some nice political maneuvering himself, Roosevelt assured Platt that he would not attack the party machine if elected.

Platt should have recognized an empty promise when he heard one. Roosevelt was elected by a slim 18,000 votes and largely ignored Platt thereafter.

TR was a good governor. With a West African proverb, "Speak softly and carry a big stick; you will go far," as his motto, he brought in a whirl of reforms. Corrupt politicians were thrown out, sweatshop regulations were tightened, the workday for women and children was shortened. But the thing that really made Platt angry was the tax on corporation franchises. These were special licenses to big companies granting them certain tax privileges. The companies had been having a field day in

New York State, using favoritism and good old paybacks to be awarded certain jobs. But this was to be no more.

Now Platt was really angry. "Get that troublemaker out of my state!" he thundered. But how? The people thought he was great. The nation thought he was a hero. Of course! That was the answer. Let the nation have him! McKinley's vice president had died in office. We'll make Roosevelt vice president!

Not so fast, however. In the first place, President McKinley didn't like TR and didn't want him on the ticket, which is the list of candidates for public office. In the second place, Marcus "Mark" Hanna, the Republican national chairman, couldn't stand him. "Don't you realize there is only one life between this madman [meaning TR] and the White House?" Hanna said. In the third place, Roosevelt didn't want the job. "I will not accept under any circumstances and that is all there is about it." Famous last words.

Roosevelt was not the first nor the last to discover that one's name on the national ticket is a powerful magnet. McKinley and Roosevelt swept the election. McKinley campaigned little, but TR ran all over the country in his colorful, explosive way, making friends and gathering voters. His popularity greatly increased the President's margin of victory.

Trouble is, once in office, Vice President Theodore Roosevelt was just plain bored—a complaint surely felt if not uttered by many vice presidents since. Second best certainly wasn't his style, and there just wasn't much to do as vice president. Some say there still isn't. Boredom went out the window, however, on September 13, 1901. TR was camping with his family in the Adirondack Mountains of New York when he got word that the President was near death. McKinley had been shot by an assassin eight days earlier in Buffalo but had seemed to be recovering. However, by the time TR got there, President McKinley was dead. On September 14, 1901, in Buffalo, New York, Theodore Roosevelt was sworn in as the twenty-sixth President of the United States.

He was 42 years old, the youngest man ever to become President. John F. Kennedy, in 1960, was the youngest ever elected President—so far. "Now look," said a dismayed Mark Hanna, "that darn cowboy is President of the United States!"

Although the cowboy announced that there would be no change at the White House, that quickly proved to be just another "campaign promise." For one thing, it was soon clear that more than anyone before him, Roosevelt loved being President. He enjoyed his new role immensely. Explorers and artists and prizefighters appeared on the dinner guest lists and government positions were filled with young college graduates. TR championed physical fitness and did daily pushups. He read the works of seventeenth-century poet John Milton and played football on the White House lawn. He was everywhere, the center of everything. A family member once said with a sigh, "When Theodore attends a wedding, he wants to be the bride, and when he attends a funeral he wants to be the corpse."

The entire White House suddenly exploded with activity. It was Roosevelt mania! The presidential kids kept a pet kangaroo, shinned up the flagpole on the White House lawn, and roller-skated on the polished wood floors. TR was often photographed with them. Said one White House staff member, "You must always remember that the president is about six."

Mrs. Roosevelt wasn't idle either. The White House was a mess. Years of traipsing in and out had weakened the floors, there were no closets, all the wiring was faulty, and bathrooms were far too few. She wanted some repairs and her husband agreed. Someone suggested it would be cheaper to tear down the whole place and start again. TR wouldn't hear of it. The White House was a living symbol of the country, and it would stay. Congress approved nearly $500,000 to fix it up in June 1902.

The White House was remodeled, rearranged, and reconstructed into basically what it looks like today. Business callers enter to the west, social callers through the East Wing, and family and guest entrances are on the north and south. The Roosevelts moved back in November 1902. But more than a renovation had occurred. Known officially as the White House since 1901, it was no longer just the President's home or the President's office. It had become the official residence of the United States of America, perhaps not quite as "homey" as before, but now with a sense of dignity and grandeur befitting a proud nation.

Roosevelt came to power at a time of unrest in the country. Workers, farmers, and labor unions were crying out for reform of bad working conditions and economic depressions. They often felt unfairly treated by the big and powerful corporations. In Roosevelt, they had a progressive leader. Although there were other progressive legislators in government, TR knew that Congress was controlled by conservative Republicans. He saw the way to reform not through laws passed by Congress but through the use of his own executive power.

A man of wealth and privilege, Roosevelt put the prestige of the presidency behind the attack on the "criminal rich." Shortly after taking office, he stopped the Northern Securities Company from creating a monopoly, or taking total control, over railroad transportation in the northwest. He did this by reviving the all-but-forgotten Sherman Antitrust Act of 1890, which made it illegal to limit, or restrain, interstate and foreign trade.

A 1904 cartoon shows Roosevelt wielding a big stick at an assortment of monopolies including the railroad, beef, and oil trusts, and "Everything in General."

During his term of office he would continue to "bust" monopolies. Through the office of the attorney general of the United States, charges were brought against 43 other corporations for violating antitrust laws.

In May 1902 Roosevelt ran up against the biggest challenge to his entire presidency. The United Mine Workers called their 150,000 men out on strike. They wanted better wages and working conditions. The mine owners backed by the railroads would not negotiate.

Roosevelt traveled about the country urging both sides to talk. Management told TR to mind his own business. Now he really got mad. He let it be known that he would call in the army to run the mines. The startled owners agreed to talk, the workers agreed to go back to the mines, and they eventually won a modest pay increase. It was the first time the federal government had interfered in a labor struggle in this way.

Although labor leaders were upset by TR's threat of the army, he was a hero again to many working people. Said he, "All I wanted was to see to it that every man has a square deal, no more and no less." The term "square deal" stuck and he used it to bring about a number of domestic reforms. The Department of Commerce and Labor was established to look out for the welfare of American workers through laws and special programs. The Elkins Act compelled the railroads to stick to their agreed-upon charges for carrying freight. The Expedition Act meant quicker trials for those who broke antitrust laws. A lover of the outdoors, Roosevelt pushed the Reclamation Act of 1902. It called for building dams and irrigating dry land areas in some western states. He enlarged the Bureau of Forestry. Thousands of acres of timberland were set aside for national use, national parks were doubled, game preserves were established.

TR was also looking beyond U.S. borders. He made no secret of the fact that he wanted the United States to expand. One of his dreams was to build a canal across Central America. He got what he wanted but it got him in trouble, too. The United States wanted to build a canal linking the Atlantic and Pacific Oceans in a neutral zone. In June 1902, Congress gave the President permission to construct a canal across Panama, which was then part of Colombia in Central America. First, however, TR had to get Colombia's permanent okay for U.S. control of the canal. Although in a convention Colombia agreed, its legislature voted against it in August 1903. TR began making noises about losing his patience. In a most convenient happening, Panama declared itself independent two months later, nudged most said by U.S. interests. While the U.S. Navy quickly stood guard in Panama, Colombian troops sent to put down the revolt were

Roosevelt visits a Panama Canal construction site in 1906.

bribed to ignore it. With amazing speed, the United States recognized the new country and paid $10 million plus $250,000 annually for a canal zone ten miles wide.

It was a rather obvious display of power, causing lots of bad feelings toward the United States for many years. TR was undisturbed. "I took the Canal Zone, and let Congress debate, and while the debate goes on, the canal does also." It cost $380 million and took 43,000 workers to build the Panama Canal. Many workers fell to the dread diseases of malaria and yellow fever, although both were generally wiped out in the region by the end of the project. The canal opened to traffic in 1920. After much controversy, the Canal Zone was transferred to Panamanian control in 1979.

In 1904, Theodore Roosevelt's Square Deal got him elected to four years of his own as President, with Senator Charles Warren

Fairbanks of Indiana as vice president. Roosevelt beat out the rather dull Democrat Alton B. Parker, 336 electoral votes to 140.

Much of what Roosevelt accomplished in office was important because it paved the way for others to follow. But he did much in many areas too. He settled a dispute with Canada over the Alaskan boundary. He proved he could be a diplomat. In 1905, he mediated an agreement between Japan and Russia in their squabble over Manchuria and Korea. For that he won the Nobel Peace Prize in 1906. The prize money of more than $36,000 went into a fund for industrial peace, but during World War I, the money was channeled to aid war victims. He signed the Pure Food and Drug Act and the Meat Inspection Act in 1906. Meat packing houses and stockyards now had to pass inspection. Americans still benefit from those acts today. Among other things, they made labeling honest. Also in 1906, the Hepburn Act regulated railroad rates. When Californians, fearful for their jobs, turned hostile over the number of Japanese immigrants and Japan in turn grew furious over the treatment of its people in America, TR reached a "gentleman's agreement" in 1907. The Japanese would slow down emigration, and the United States would not pass a law limiting the number of Japanese allowed into the United States.

TR was the first U.S. President to win the Nobel Peace Prize, but he was "first" in other ways as well. He was the first to invite an African American—educator Booker T. Washington—to a White House dinner. He was the first to leave the United States while in office when he went to the Panama Canal site. He organized the first White House Press Room. He was the first to fly (1910) and, in fact, set up the U.S. Army Air Forces when he bought a plane from the Wright Brothers for $25,000. He was also the first vice president to be elected on his own and the first Republican President from the East. Last and perhaps least, he was the first to use the oft-quoted expression "my hat is in the ring," meaning a politician is about to run for office.

When his two terms were over, TR stepped down, endorsing William Howard Taft as his successor. Almost immediately he left on a hunting trip to Africa. Still the people's favorite, he returned to a smashing parade down Fifth Avenue in New York City. To no one's surprise, his retirement to his home in Oyster Bay, New York, didn't last long. Angry because Taft wouldn't follow his advice on everything, Roosevelt turned radical. "My hat is in the ring," he declared. "The fight is on." The Republicans were not impressed by his colorful speech and renominated Taft in 1912. That made Roosevelt so angry that he bolted the party and became the candidate of a third party, the Progressives. It was sometimes called the Bull Moose party after TR declared prior to running, "I am fit as a bull moose."

A contemporary cartoon by C. Budd in 1917 shows Teddy Roosevelt inviting voters into his Progressive party (Bull Moose) wigwam.

If TR wanted revenge on Taft, he got it, but he brought down his old party in the process. He received more votes than Taft. However, neither man got back into office. With the Republicans split, the Democrats breezed into the White House with Woodrow Wilson.

Still not ready for retirement, TR asked the new President to let him put together a regiment to fight in World War I. Referring to Roosevelt's age and "lack of discipline," Wilson said no. TR proved himself as vengeful as ever. He later helped to destroy Wilson's League of Nations, forerunner of the United Nations.

Saddened by the death in France of his aviator son, Quentin, TR entered the hospital on Armistice Day, November 11, 1918. World War I was over, and the fight was almost gone from the old colonel, too. He died of a heart attack on January 6, 1919.

TR seems to have been larger than life. But he also had his critics. Many people, especially his enemies, said he was pushy. He probably was. For all his jovial ways, he was undoubtedly arrogant. To disagree with him was on about the same level as committing a federal crime. His anger was rare but, apparently, fearsome. Although he was hailed as a crusader for the people, there is little evidence that he was truly concerned with racial issues and, in fact, was said to feel that some races were, indeed, superior to others.

But for all these detractions, the bottom line is: Was Theodore Roosevelt a good President? Did he make a difference? The answer is yes. Most historians rank him fairly high on the list of effective men in the White House. He believed with all his heart in a strong presidency. "The efficiency of the Government," he said, "depends upon its possessing a strong central executive, and wherever I could establish a precedent for strength in the executive...I have felt...that I was establishing a precedent of value."

And most would agree that he did. By the force of his personality and his convictions, he changed the role of the presidency. Many who came after him remembered his lesson. He was TR, the man who carried a big stick into the White House and also gave us the teddy bear.

Names in the News in Roosevelt's Time

John Jacob Astor (1864–1912):

Great-grandson of Astor tycoon (1763–1848), fought in Spanish-American War, died along with some 1,500 others when luxury liner *Titanic* was hit by an iceberg and sunk.

William Edward Burghardt Du Bois (1868–1963):

Harvard graduate, African American professor of economics and history, Atlanta University.

(continued on next page)

Henry Ford (1863–1947):

Born on Michigan farm, began experimenting with engines as apprentice in Detroit, age 16. Built first motor vehicle (1896), organized Ford Motor Company (1903). First "Model T" (1909). Perfected the assembly line—a system of mass production. Instituted eight-hour workday, (1914). Sent peace ship to Europe to try to stop World War I (1915).

In 1916, cartoonist T.E. Powers depicted Henry Ford's return to the U.S. from his futile peace mission to end World War I.

George Washington Goethals (1858–1928):

West Point graduate, commanded Panama Canal construction. Hailed as genius of "greatest engineering feat of the ages."

Bat Masterson (1853–1921):

Real name William Barclay Masterson, sports writer, scout, sheriff, U.S. marshal in western frontier towns.

Jacob Riis (1849–1914):

Born in Denmark, journalist. Worked for improved schools and tenements in New York City; coworker with TR.

Ida Tarbell (1857–1944):

American author, born in Pennsylvania. Wrote of working oppressed in such titles as *The Business of Being a Woman* (1912) and *New Ideals in Business* (1916).

Wilbur and Orville Wright (1867–1912, 1871–1948)

Aviation pioneers and bicycle manufacturers from Ohio. Made a few successful engine-powered flights, one was 59 seconds, 852 feet, on December 17, 1903, Kitty Hawk, North Carolina; received patent (1906).

Chapter Two

Taft: The Reluctant President

William H. Taft (1909-1913)

*W*illiam Howard Taft, who followed Teddy Roosevelt into the White House, was the first President to use the now famous Oval Office. It was added to the West Wing in 1909. He also may have been the first, and only, President who did not really want to be President. He wasn't happy in that job and he didn't much like politics in general. What he really wanted was to be a judge. However, he allowed his name on the Republican ticket in 1908 and, with Roosevelt's support, became the twenty-seventh President of the United States.

Taft was an honest, kind, and straightforward sort of man. And at well over 300 pounds, he was the largest person ever to become President. According to the story, he once got stuck in the White House bathtub. A bigger model was ordered.

With the White House in Taft's time beginning to look much as it does today, Washington, D.C., also began to take on a look that late-twentieth-century Americans would recognize. The elegant and gorgeous cherry trees that border the Potomac River in spring began to bloom. Taft was the first President to ride around town in that twentieth-century miracle—the automobile. Actually, he ordered four "horseless carriages" to be housed in the former stable: a White steamer, a Baker electric, and two Pierce Arrows. Taft was also the first President to play golf and to toss out the ball to begin the baseball season. He was, however, the last President to have a cow graze on the White House lawn. Her name was Pauline Wayne.

Pauline may well have been the only cow that grazed on a Taft lawn. The future President was not born on a farm or in a log cabin. He did not walk miles to school and his parents were not poor. His father was a lawyer and his birthplace was Cincinnati, Ohio. Taft thus became the sixth President from the Buckeye State.

William was born on September 15, 1857. His mother, Louise Torrey Taft of Boston, was from an old English family that had settled in Massachusetts in the seventeenth century. His father, Alphonso, originally from Vermont, was not only a lawyer and a diplomat, but also attorney general and secretary of war for President Ulysses S. Grant. William had two brothers, Henry and Horace, a sister, Frances, and two half brothers from his father's first marriage, Charles and Peter.

William Howard Taft may not have been our greatest President —most historians rank him as "average"—but he may well have been the most jovial. He grew up to be a very congenial and popular fellow. He was a welcome partner at dances for, despite his size, he was quite light on his feet and took dance lessons twice a week. His skill on the dance floor did not extend to the baseball diamond, however, for although he was a power hitter and a good second baseman, he was a very poor runner.

Between dances and sports, fun-loving Taft found time to be a good student. He graduated second in his class from Woodward High in 1874 and second in his class, out of 132 students, from Yale in 1878. A classmate said he was "the most admired and respected man...in all Yale."

Back in Cincinnati, Taft worked in his father's law office and entered Cincinnati Law School, graduating in 1880. By that time, he was already in politics. He helped his father campaign— unsuccessfully—for the Ohio governor's seat. Although he remained active in local politics for the next few years, he decided that he would be best suited as a judge and set his eyes on the U.S. Supreme Court. In 1890, President Benjamin Harrison called him to Washington as solicitor general, the federal government's lawyer who argues cases before the Supreme Court.

When Taft went to Washington, his wife of four years, Helen "Nellie" Herron, accompanied him. A graduate of Cincinnati College of Music, she had met Taft at a bobsledding party years before. Ambitious and intelligent, Nellie encouraged her husband in his career, having decided that the man she would marry would someday become President.

In 1891, Taft got an appointment to a new judgeship on the Sixth U.S. Circuit Court of Appeals. Nellie tried to talk him out of it because it meant leaving Washington. She was afraid that would put him out of the spotlight on the way to the presidency. But Taft insisted and performed well. He was the first judge to flatly declare that workers had a right to strike and often sided with laborers on injury cases caused by employer negligence.

Just when it looked as though a coveted seat on the Supreme Court was around the corner, fate stepped in. President McKinley asked Taft to go to the Philippine Islands, recently annexed in the Spanish-American War, to establish a government there. Neither Nellie nor Taft wanted to go this time. She for the same reason as before and he because he hated heat—and the Philippines Islands are hot! But duty called, and besides, McKinley promised him a seat on the Supreme Court when he got back. So the Tafts, now with three children, went to the Philippines in 1901 on a one-year tour and remained three years.

Taft poses for a portrait as governor of the Philippines.

Despite the heat, Taft did well in the Philippines. He quickly organized a government, negotiated with the Catholic Church to allow Filipino farmers to purchase church-owned land, set up schools and courts, and tried to open trade for the islands' products. In fact, he got so involved with the welfare of the Philippines that when now President Roosevelt called him to the Supreme Court, Taft wouldn't go! He felt responsible for the islands' welfare.

But Roosevelt knew what he wanted, and what he wanted was Will Taft. They had become friends when Taft was solicitor general. The energetic, demanding President needed a thoroughly competent administrator and a "faithful follower." That was Taft. So, instead of a seat on the bench, Roosevelt named Taft as his secretary of war. From that post, he could still oversee the welfare of the Philippines. Taft agreed and returned home.

And what a busy war secretary he was! Besides overseeing the Philippines, he was acting secretary of state for a year when John Hay became ill. He traveled to Japan and to the site of the Panama Canal construction. He went to Cuba to negotiate peace on that revolution-torn island. And most reluctantly, he turned down an appointment to the Supreme Court in January 1906. He really felt it his duty to complete his work in his present post.

The election of 1908 was fast approaching. Roosevelt would not run again. Taft was a logical choice. Roosevelt and Nellie certainly thought so, and so did many other Republican leaders. Taft didn't. Just how much they disagreed can be seen in this oft-quoted story. One evening at the White House, President Roosevelt is said to have shut his eyes and said as though in a trance, " I have clairvoyant powers. I see a man weighing 350 pounds. There is something hanging over his head...at one time it looks like the presidency, then again it looks like the chief justiceship." Nellie said, "Make it the presidency." Taft said, "Make it the chief justiceship."

The presidency it was. In the election of 1908, with James Schoolcraft Sherman of New York as his running mate, Taft beat the Democratic nominee, William Jennings Bryan, by more than one million votes. It was an impressive show, 321 electoral votes to 162, but it was really Roosevelt's victory. With his great popularity and charismatic personality, TR controlled the Republican

*A banner proclaiming the Republican candidacy of Taft
and Sherman flies over a New York City street in 1908.*

convention and secured the nomination for Taft. By making sure
that the entire country knew whom TR favored, he also practically won the election for him.

William Howard Taft may have entered the White House
somewhat reluctantly, but Nellie Taft was immensely pleased.
She was the first First Lady to ride with her husband along
Pennsylvania Avenue on Inauguration Day. Before that, the
new President had just been accompanied by the old one.
Unfortunately, two months after the Tafts moved into the White
House, the First Lady suffered a stroke that impaired her speech.
However, with the help of her sister and daughter, she was able
to do some entertaining and was a gracious hostess. She was also
responsible for the planting of the 3,000 Japanese cherry trees

around the Tidal Basin in the nation's capital. Nellie Taft lived until 1943 and is buried beside her husband at Arlington National Cemetery.

After Taft's election, Teddy Roosevelt had written: "Taft will carry on the work substantially as I have...he will persevere in every one of the great governmental policies in which I most firmly believe." In short, a contemporary historian said, "Taft will be me!" But, of course, Taft wasn't Roosevelt. Never could be, never wanted to be, and never really wanted to be President. Will Taft walked into the Oval Office an unhappy man and stayed that way for nearly all of his four years as chief executive. Even with the presidential salary raised to $75,000, friendly Will soon discovered that the top of the heap can be "the loneliest place in the world." That's what he called the White House.

The new President was well aware that he lacked Roosevelt's star quality. He knew his administration would be quieter and slower and that the public would miss the grand show that TR had put on. Taft was not a creative or even a forceful leader. He was, however, an earnest man with the intelligence to know his limitations and the will to do well by his country. If his record is not spectacular, it is honest, and he did have some accomplishments. He strongly enforced antitrust laws and backed conservation practices. He struggled against big business to get a slight reduction in tariffs through Congress. An able administrator, he saved the government millions of dollars

A Taft family photograph taken on the White House porch. President and Mrs. Taft are seated with Charles P., Helen, and Robert Taft (left to right) standing behind them.

by keeping a close watch on spending. During his four years, New Mexico and Arizona were admitted to the Union, bringing the total to 48 states, and the Sixteenth Amendment was ratified. Now Congress could collect income taxes!

In foreign affairs, Taft was not so successful. He angered other nations by announcing that since the United States had built the Panama Canal, U.S. ships would not have to pay tolls when using it. Trouble was, the United States had already signed a treaty stating that all countries would pay equally. President Wilson later reversed Taft's ruling. In 1911, Taft forced a treaty with Canada through Congress to lower tariffs between the two countries. But Canada had second thoughts and refused to sign it. Taft was also disappointed in his attempts to get foreign countries to agree to submit disputes that might lead to war to a higher authority, such as the International Court at The Hague in the Netherlands.

But the biggest headache of Taft's administration was at home. Because his true interest was not in politics but in the courts, Taft failed to see the growing split in his own party between conservatives and progressives. He became puzzled when his old friend TR, who was becoming ever more radical on issues, began to speak out against Taft's more moderate policies. As Roosevelt became more angry, Taft grew more sorrowful but refused to respond. Finally, and reluctantly, he had to take a stand. He decided to run for reelection.

With the Republican party split by TR's running on the Progressive ticket, Taft's election was doomed. Democrat Woodrow Wilson swept in. Taft got only eight electoral votes in the election. If that made him unhappy, it was hard to tell. Rarely has a candidate been less disappointed by losing an election! "The nearer I get to the inauguration of my successor, the greater the relief I feel," said Taft. And so it was a contented man, at age 55, who stepped out of the Oval Office in March 1913 and headed for private life.

In private life, Taft actually began to lose some weight. His size had always brought some kidding in the national press and he was generally good-natured about it. Once when he was in the Philippines, then Secretary of War Elihu Root had inquired about his health. Taft said he had just ridden for miles into the hills and he felt fine. Root cabled back, "But how is the horse?" Just out of the White House, Yale University offered him the Kent Chair of Constitutional Law. Taft did go to Yale for a time. However, he said he couldn't take the chair but a "sofa of law" would be fine.

What he actually got—finally and at long last—was his dream. After serving as chairman of the National War Labor Board during World War I, William Howard Taft was appointed Chief Justice of the U.S. Supreme Court. President Warren G. Harding so named him in June 1921. Will Taft was a happy man.

Happy he remained for nine years. Taft is the only man to serve both as President of the United States and Chief Justice of the Supreme Court. Immediately, he used his vast administrative skills to clear up the Court's impossibly cluttered and clogged caseload. In 1925, he secured passage of the Judges Act. This allowed the Court to have a wider say in what cases it would hear so that it could concentrate, as it does today, on those involving interpretation of the U.S. Constitution. In all, Taft wrote 253 opinions, mostly conservative and middle-of-the-

Taft photographed in his robes as Chief Justice of the Supreme Court in the early 1920s.

road decisions, during his time on the bench. To "sit on the bench" means to be a judge in a court. His most lasting contribution was his opinion in *Myers v. United States* (1926). An opinion in this sense means the legal reasons upon which a judge bases his or her decisions. The *Myers* case made the 1867

Tenure of Office Act unconstitutional and upheld presidential authority to remove federal officials. It was Andrew Johnson's violation of the Tenure Act that brought impeachment charges against him in 1868.

With Nellie in better health and his own form as trim as it would ever be, Taft enjoyed his years on the bench and worked hard. But, finally, high blood pressure and heart disease began to impair his ability to serve. In February 1930, he was forced to retire due to poor health. A month later, at his home in Washington, D.C., the twenty-seventh President of the United States died in his sleep. He is buried at Arlington National Cemetery, one of only two U.S. Presidents to be buried there. The other is John F. Kennedy.

Taft was not an outstanding President by almost any method of comparison. Some thought him lacking in the forcefulness and leadership that the Oval Office demands. And perhaps so. He was, however, a most able administrator. His term in office may have been unspectacular and he may have been a reluctant leader, but Taft gave his country four years of government that was as honest as he knew how to make it. For any President in any age, that's just about as good as it gets.

Names in the News in Taft's Time

Jane Addams (1860–1935):

Born in Illinois, social reformer and peace advocate. Established and ran Hull Settlement House (Chicago) with Ellen Gates Starr (1889–1935). Shared Nobel Peace Prize (1931).

Louis Brandeis (1856–1941):

Kentucky-born jurist. Heavily involved in labor law. Associate justice U.S. Supreme Court (1916–1939).

William Jennings Bryan (1860–1925):

Lawyer and political leader from Illinois, known as "The Commoner." Nominated three times for President, third defeat by Taft. Secretary of state under Wilson. Prosecuting attorney in famous Tennessee case against John T. Scopes (1925), accused of teaching evolution in his classes. Defense counsel Clarence Darrow exposed Bryan's ignorance of scientific discoveries.

Shortly after the close of the Scopes "monkey" trial, an American newspaper ran this cartoon showing the two opposing lawyers, William Jennings Bryan (left) and Clarence Darrow (right), shaking hands.

Ty (Tyrus Raymond) Cobb (1886–1961):

Baseball Hall of Famer known as the "Georgia Peach"; 22 seasons as Detroit Tigers outfielder (1904–26); lifetime batting average: .367.

Oliver Wendell Holmes, Jr. (1841–1935):

American jurist, Harvard graduate, Civil War veteran. Associate justice U.S. Supreme Court (1902–1932). Established "clear and present danger" as the only basis for restricting freedom of speech.

Chapter Three

Wilson the Peacemaker

Woodrow Wilson (1913-1921)

A scholar...a teacher...an orator...a governor... a President...a peacemaker...a slow learner! Who was this man?

His name was Thomas Woodrow Wilson. He was all those things. He would grow up to become the twenty-eighth President of the United States, and a great one as well.

Wilson was indeed an intelligent, articulate scholar, a professor of history, president of Princeton University, and a most successful governor of New Jersey. He was a gifted, moving speaker before large crowds and a shy awkward mumbler in small ones. His long face was rather homely. He had big ears and poor eyesight. His teachers said he was a slow learner, and in fact, he didn't read until the age of nine. Once he got the hang of it, however, he couldn't be slowed down!

Woodrow Wilson—he dropped his first name after college — devoted his life, his administration, and his health to the cause of international peace. He lost his health and never achieved his cause. It is ironic that this man, who led the United States through World War I, is remembered not for the war he won but for the peace he lost.

Born on December 28, 1856, he was the eighth and, to date, last President born in Virginia. His father, Joseph Ruggles Wilson, was a Presbyterian minister. His mother, the former Janet Woodrow, was born in England and had the reputation of being cranky. Her son adored her. When he was about a year old, the family, including two older sisters and a younger brother, moved from his birthplace in Staunton, Virginia, to Augusta, Georgia, and later to Columbia, South Carolina, and Wilmington, North Carolina. Some of his earliest and most lasting recollections were of the devastation caused by the Civil War. He believed in the Southern cause. Although he spent all of his adult life in the North, he would always regard himself as a Southerner.

As a child, Wilson was thought to be a slow learner, having trouble with reading and math. He was a frail boy with poor eyesight and wore glasses from the time he was eight years old. But by the time he was 16, he had progressed so well in his studies that he entered Davidson College in North Carolina. Poor health forced him out after a year. In 1875, he was healthy again and entered the College of New Jersey at Princeton. Wilson graduated thirty-eighth in his 1879 class of 167 students. Although he still hated math, he loved the debating team and was a valuable member of it.

Poor health overtook him again, forcing him to leave the University of Virginia Law School in his second year. Even though he was still far more interested in debating than in law, he completed his studies at home and passed the bar exam. After a brief fling at a law practice in Atlanta, he decided on a new career, and it changed his life. In 1883, Wilson entered graduate school at Johns Hopkins University in Baltimore, Maryland. Two years later, his book, *Congressional Government: A Study in American Politics*, was published. In it, he condemned the way Congress dominated the executive and judicial branches of government. The President of the United States, wrote Wilson, is a mere figurehead. His book brought him much acclaim and set him on his career path. In 1886, he earned a doctoral degree in political science. Wilson is the only U.S. President with a PhD.

On June 24, 1885, at the age of 28, Woodrow Wilson married Ellen Louise Axson of Georgia. Theirs was a happy marriage,

During his first term as President, Woodrow Wilson poses with his first wife, Ellen, and their three daughters (left to right) Margaret, Eleanor, and Jessie. Eleanor and Jessie were married in the White House within eight months—November 1913 to July 1914.

which produced three daughters, two of whom would be married in the White House.

Until the late 1880s, Wilson taught at Bryn Mawr College in Pennsylvania and at Wesleyan University in Connecticut, where he also coached the football team. In 1890, he happily accepted a full professorship at his beloved College of New Jersey in Princeton, named for William III, prince of Orange-Nassau and king of England. The school was renamed Princeton University in 1896. His academic reputation on the rise, Wilson published a number of scholarly books and articles before he was elected president of Princeton in 1902.

The new president had some immediate success, especially at reorganizing the university's course of studies. But he also had a big defeat. It was such a little thing, but it demonstrated the flaw that would bring about his greatest failure as president. Woodrow Wilson was a stubborn man, high-minded and often inflexible. This particular issue concerned whether the new Princeton graduate school should be located on or off campus. Wilson wanted it on campus and under his control. He would not compromise. The fight went on for two years and ended only because Princeton was offered several million dollars on the condition that the graduate facility would be off campus. Wilson had to give in. A few months later, in October 1910, he resigned.

By that time, he was bored anyway. He had been bitten by the political bug. With his ideas changing from conservative to progressive, Wilson was chosen to run for the governorship of New Jersey in 1910. The Democratic party bosses recognized a popular figure when they saw one. They also recognized a political rookie. What they wanted was a well-known face with no political baggage, someone who would not upset party organization. In other words, the party bosses wanted to stay in control. They figured the inexperienced Wilson to be their man. Wilson calmly assured the bosses that he would not upset their political applecart and plunged into the race. He won easily and found, to his surprise, that he liked campaigning.

The party bosses were happy—but not for long. Candidate Wilson was a different cup of tea from Governor Wilson. Vowing to "lance the bosses like warts," he startled nearly everyone by almost immediately starting reforms. These included workmen's compensation laws, reorganization of elections, and regulation of public utilities. The new governor of New Jersey was hailed as an independent, progressive leader. That was his first year in office. In his second year, however, he ran into trouble. The Republicans gained control of both houses of the state legislature. Once again, Wilson's personality got in the way. He simply would not compromise and ended up vetoing 57 measures. It was his way or no way. Wilson had to go it alone. It was the only way he knew, said a later historian.

Even before he was elected governor, Democratic leaders had planned on running Wilson in the presidential election of 1912. But after his second year as governor, they weren't so sure. In fact, Wilson very nearly lost the nomination. The Democratic National Convention was pretty well split among Wilson, Speaker of the House Champ Clark of Missouri, and Oscar W. Underwood from Alabama. But Wilson hung in and, on the forty-sixth ballot, was declared the Democratic nominee. Thomas R. Marshall of Indiana became his running mate.

According to the old saying, timing is everything. It certainly was in this case. Although it didn't seem so at first glance, Democrat Wilson could not have picked a better time to run. The Republicans already had their man—William Howard Taft—in the White House. The people liked him and he was running again. By all rights, he should have been an easy winner. But the Republican party was in confusion because the former and still popular President, Teddy Roosevelt, had gone over to the Progressives. While Taft sat on his front porch for most of the campaign, TR ran around the country gathering attention and votes. In so doing, he split the Republican voters, and in walked the Democrat, Thomas Woodrow Wilson, twenty-eighth President of the United States. The count was was 435 electoral votes for Wilson, 88 for TR, and 8 for Taft.

The new President had called for reform during his campaign. Now he actually began to do what he had promised! That was stunning in itself. First, he revived a practice that had died with President John Adams. Wilson delivered his first message to Congress in person, a custom still followed today in the President's State of the Union speech each January. Then he got down to business.

Wilson's accomplishments during his first two years in office are impressive. His first major legislation was the Underwood Tariff Act. It reduced high duties on foreign imports—much to the anger of American industry. High tariffs had been imposed during the nineteenth century to protect new and weak American companies against the wealthier and more established European concerns. But now, with American industry thriving, such high duties tended to raise the cost of living to the average U.S. worker.

Congress also passed a federal income tax, which the Sixteenth Amendment, ratified during Taft's term, allowed it to do. The Seventeenth Amendment was passed in 1913. It called for the direct election of U.S. senators. In late 1913, the Federal Reserve Act created the Federal Reserve Board to regulate Federal Reserve banks and control currency. The following year the Federal Trade Commission was established, giving the federal government the power to assure fair conditions of competition in trade. Also in 1914, the Clayton Antitrust Act strengthened labor organizations by legalizing boycotts and strikes. In 1916, Wilson pushed Congress to pass a bill fixing an eight-hour day for trainmen, paving the way for a general eight-hour workday.

All these measures created a new economic as well as social atmosphere in the country. However, in many ways the reform-minded Wilson stayed with his conservative roots. Blacks and whites were still segregated in government offices, with the President's approval. He drew the anger of American women by repeatedly refusing to back those who called for an amendment to give women the vote. He had favored women's rights during his campaign, but now used the excuse that the Democratic platform, a statement of party policies, had not approved it. The Nineteenth Amendment barring voting discrimination on account of sex was finally passed in August 1920. He refused to sign a child-labor law in 1914 because he said it was unconstitutional.

However, with his impressive record of reform, the President grew ever more confident and comfortable in his role as chief of state. He liked the White House. He liked being President. He acted almost as though this was his destiny. Such high-mindedness sometimes can be the spur that gets things done. It can also lead to a mighty fall. In Wilson's case, it did both.

But first came the tragedy of his wife's death, on August 6, 1914, just five days after World War I had begun in Europe. She

President Wilson and his future second wife, Mrs. Edith Bolling Galt (with corsage), attending the 1915 World Series in Philadelphia. Mayor Blankenburg of Philadelphia stands to the right.

had been slow to recover from a fall a few months earlier and had been diagnosed with kidney disease. Wilson was so upset that he told an aide he hoped to be assassinated. News of the President's depression worried the White House doctor, Cary T. Grayson, who became concerned about his mental state. Grayson was responsible for introducing Edith Bolling Galt, an attractive, intelligent Washington widow, to the President. Wilson proposed marriage the following May, but the engagement was kept secret until October. By then the gossip had already begun. Papers blasted the lack of respect shown for his wife by another marriage so soon. There were even hints that Wilson and Galt had murdered the First Lady! Against the press onslaught, Wilson offered Galt the opportunity to back out, but she refused. The 58-year-old President and the 43-year-old great-granddaughter of Pocahontas were married quietly on December 18, 1915. "She seemed to come into our life here like a special gift from Heaven," said Wilson. The two remained devoted until the end of his life. After he suffered a stroke in 1919, Edith Wilson played a significant role in the operation of the government.

Wilson had been deeply involved in American issues, but now foreign affairs would occupy most of his time. With the outbreak of World War I in August 1914, Woodrow Wilson would experience his most severe test, his greatest victory, and his most bitter failure.

The war began in Europe after a 19-year-old nationalist in Sarajevo, a city under Austrian control, assassinated Archduke Francis Ferdinand of Austria-Hungary on June 28, 1914. Sarajevo would become part of Yugoslavia in 1918 and the capital city of Bosnia and Herzegovina when the Yugoslav republic broke up in the early 1990s. But the true cause of the war was the militant nationalism that had been mounting in Europe for decades. The Allied Powers—Great Britain, France, Italy, Russia, Japan, Portugal, some Latin American countries, China, and Greece—were opposed by the Central Powers—Germany, Austria-Hungary, Bulgaria, and Turkey. (See Some American Heroes of World War I, page 49.)

First and foremost, President Wilson was determined to keep America out of the war. And, in truth, in 1914, the United States was ill prepared to fight a large-scale battle. But it was an uneasy neutrality. Most Americans, because of cultural ties, favored the British and French. But large groups of vocal minorities backed Germany and Austria-Hungary. Wilson offered to mediate peace terms between the warring parties but to no avail.

In fact, Germany grew ever more belligerent. The German Embassy in Washington, D.C., published a newspaper ad in early May warning travelers that a state of war existed between Germany and Great Britain and its allies. On

The torpedoing of the British liner Lusitania *by a German U-boat on May 7, 1915, almost caused Wilson to declare war.*

May 1, 1915, a German submarine, known as a U-boat, sunk an American merchant ship, and on May 6, two British merchant ships went down. Wilson stood firm on neutrality. Then, on May 7, his neutral stand very nearly collapsed. A German U-boat torpedoed the British liner *Lusitania* off the coast of Ireland. Of the nearly 1,200 who died, 128 were Americans.

The shocked American public began to call for war. Wilson still would not budge. In fact, he gave a most unfortunate speech in Philadelphia a few days later. He said, "There is such a thing as a man being too proud to fight. There is such a thing as a nation being so right that it does not need to convince others by force that it is right." This made it sound as though he were calling for "peace at any price," no matter what the other side did. However, Wilson did strongly protest the sinking to Germany, which promised not to attack unarmed liners, a promise not kept for long.

Yet, it was kept long enough to put Wilson back in the White House after the 1916 election. His campaign slogan was "He kept us out of war." Even so, the election was very close against Republican and former Supreme Court Justice Charles Evans Hughes. In fact, it was so close that Hughes went to bed on election night believing he'd won because it looked like he was winning California. He didn't. According to the story, a reporter called Hughes in the morning to give him the California total. A Hughes aide said with great disdain, "The President can't be disturbed." Replied the reporter, "Well, when he wakes up, tell him he's no longer President." The electoral vote count was 277 to 254.

Hughes was apparently so miffed at the outcome that he did not send Wilson a telegram conceding the election until two weeks later. Said Wilson with a flash of humor, "It [the telegram] was a little moth-eaten...but quite legible."

One of the reasons the election was so close was the mess Wilson had made of relations with the U.S. neighbor to the south—Mexico. Without truly understanding the complex

This 1916 Democratic party election campaign van promotes items that Wilson had accomplished during the past four years and advertises the President's stand against the European war.

forces controlling the Mexican Revolution in 1913, he refused to recognize the dictatorship government of Victoriano Huerta. Instead, he set up a policy of "watchful waiting" and resisted all suggestions of sending in troops. After Huerta resigned, Venustiano Carranza took over and Wilson recognized his government in 1915. But Carranza could do little about the revolutionaries roaming the country, and in March of the following year, revolutionary leader Pancho Villa crossed the border and killed 17 Americans in New Mexico. Wilson's response was to send in 6,000 U.S. troops under General John J. Pershing, who crossed back across the border in pursuit. They never did find Villa, but they earned the wrath of Carranza for invading his country. Wilson called them back in February 1917. By that time, the only thing that had been accomplished was bitter feelings between the two countries, which lasted for decades.

Even though the 1916 election was close, Wilson took his victory as the country's support of his stand on neutrality. He was convinced by now that he could succeed as an international peacemaker. He was the man to bring both parties to the bargaining table. In a speech to Congress on January 22, 1917, he urged both warring sides to accept "peace without victory." Both sides ignored him. In fact, the Allies said they would fight to the absolute finish. Nine days later, it really didn't matter any more. Wilson's immovable stand on neutrality at all costs was about to come crashing down.

On January 31, 1917, the German ambassador announced to Secretary of State Robert Lansing that, against earlier promises, Germany was about to resume submarine torpedo raids. Wilson severed relations with Germany four days later. Still hoping to stay out of war, he asked Congress for authority to arm U.S. merchant ships, which he got on March 1. Three days later, the nation heard of the Zimmermann telegram. Dated January 16, it had been sent by German Foreign Minister Athur Zimmermann to the German ambassador in Mexico City and intercepted by the Americans. It said that if there was war between the United States and Germany, Mexico would be given land carved out of Arizona, New Mexico, and Texas.

The American public was outraged, but Wilson still wanted to "wait and see." After a few more U.S. merchant ships went down, Wilson the peacemaker had no choice but to give in. On April 2, 1917, he asked

The New York Journal *headline announces the declaration of war by the United States against Germany on April 6, 1917. Fifty members of the House of Representatives including the first woman member, Jeannette Rankin (Montana), still voted for peace.*

Congress to declare war against Germany, saying, "The present German submarine warfare against commerce is a war against mankind."

Despite his stand for neutrality, once committed, Wilson proved to be a strong and effective leader. Woefully unprepared, the United States took more than a year to reach full fighting strength. But the so-called American Expeditionary Force under General John J. Pershing, which fought in Europe independent of Allied control, was the chief mover in turning the war against the Central Powers. Although the Germans were victorious in the early months of 1918, the Allies, especially the American infantrymen known popularly as "doughboys," won the important battles of Chateau-Thierry and Belleau Wood in June, the Second Battle of the Marne in July,

During World War I, American women joined the work force to replace men and increase the production of firearms and other necessary materiel. These women are welding bomb casings in a munitions factory.

Saint-Mihiel in September, and the Meuse-Argonne offensive later that fall. The United States of America came out of World War I as a recognized world power.

The armistice that ended the war occurred officially on the eleventh hour of the eleventh day of the eleventh month— November 11, 1918. At that time, one million American troops were in Europe. Some 53,000 Americans had died in action and more than 300,000 were injured.

Wilson the peacemaker quickly announced that he would head the U.S. delegation to the peace conference in Paris. His personal emissary, Colonel Edward M. House, cabled from France saying that would be unwise. Except for T. Roosevelt's visit to Panama in 1906, no American President had ever left the country while in office, and House feared it would mean a loss of dignity. Wilson, as usual, was stubborn. He was going. He was also going without Republicans, who had gained control of both houses of Congress in the last election. Since the Senate eventually had to approve any treaty, he was urged to take some Republicans along. Wilson refused.

Woodrow Wilson was not going to the peace conference unprepared. Earlier in the year he had outlined his Fourteen Points for peace in a speech to Congress. He declared these to be the only principles on which a lasting peace could be built. Among other conditions, the Fourteen Points included open treaties with no secret agreements, freedom of navigation on the seas, arms reductions, equal trade conditions, fair adjustment of colonial claims, restoration of Belgium, and a free Poland with access to the sea.

But the self-appointed peace advocate soon realized his task would not be easy. England, France, and Italy were more interested in future security and in keeping Germany from rising

French premier, Georges Clemenceau, President Wilson, and Britain's Lloyd George (tipping his hat) leave the Hall of Mirrors at Versailles, France, after signing the peace treaty on June 28, 1919.

again than in giving up secret treaties or territorial rights. And the conditions they imposed on Germany were severe. Through the Treaty of Versailles, Germany was stripped of all colonial possessions, its armed forces were abolished, and it was forced to pay many billions of dollars in war reparations. This colossal war debt forced the Germans into almost total economic depression. But the most severe aspect of the treaty, and the one that caused the most bitterness within Germany, was the so-called war guilt clause. It forced the Germans to accept complete responsibility for starting the war. This, more than any other part of the treaty, embittered the German people. The German leaders who signed the treaty were immediately called traitors. This clause, as much as or more than the reparations, is often cited as the basis for the ugly militancy that once again sprang up in Germany with the rise of Adolf Hitler in the 1930s.

However, the Treaty of Versailles provided for something that Woodrow Wilson wanted above all else—a League of Nations. This would be a worldwide organization to promote and keep world peace. It became Wilson's dream. And because it was, he found himself giving in time and again on small points in order to keep the League as part of the eventual treaty.

Fighting among the winning powers was sometimes more like a barroom brawl than a peace convention. In July, however, Wilson returned home to offer the Treaty of Versailles for Senate approval. He said, "The stage is set, the destiny disclosed." Trouble was, the Senate was split over the League of Nations. The Democratic minority supported the treaty and the League. Some Republicans didn't want the League at all, some would sign the treaty and worry about the League later. At any rate, there weren't enough votes for ratification.

Wilson wanted the treaty signed and he wanted the League of Nations. So he set out across the country to appeal to the people. From east to west, he spoke in some 30 cities during the month of September. He was tired, worn out, frustrated, and ill.

On September 25, he suffered a slight stroke and the rest of the tour was canceled. Back in Washington, he suffered a more severe stroke on October 2 and was partially paralyzed. He never fully recovered.

Now began a unique period in U.S. history. For the next several months, few people saw or heard of the President, with the exception of his doctor and Mrs. Wilson. The President made decisions from his sickbed, or so it was said. Wilson refused to give up authority to operate the government, and no one challenged him. Practically no one even got in to see him. Was he actually running the show? No one knows for sure. For years there was speculation, and probably still is, that during that period, America had its first woman acting as President—Edith Galt Wilson. In her memoirs, she admitted that she carefully screened all matters of state that were put before the President. In other words, she may not have made the final decision, but she apparently did decide what he would see in the first place. To prevent such a situation from reoccurring, the Twenty-Fifth Amendment was ratified in 1967. It calls for the vice president to become acting President whenever the President declares, in writing, that he or she is unable to carry out the duties of the office.

Meanwhile, the fight over ratifying the peace treaty went on in the Senate. Finally, on November 6, 1919, Republican Henry Cabot Lodge of Massachusetts, chairman of the Senate Foreign Relations Committee, announced that he would endorse the treaty. It was presented for the President's signature with some minor changes—ironically, fourteen!

At last, Wilson the peacemaker had what he wanted—a treaty and a promise to build a world peace organization. So, what did he do? The President refused to sign it! In ill health or not, he was as stubborn as ever. He would not accept Lodge's reservations. The United States never signed the peace treaty that it had fought for. A separate treaty was signed with Germany in 1921 under Harding. The United States never joined the League of Nations. American absence contributed to the failure of the League, which was established with headquarters in Geneva, Switzerland, in 1920. When it failed to stop Japan from marching into Manchuria, or Italy into Ethiopia, or German military buildup in the 1930s, the League ceased to function. It was not until 1946, with the United Nations, that another organization dedicated to peace came into being. Once again, life is sometimes stranger than fiction. The very man who worked so hard for a peace organization, losing his health in the process, was the very man who kept the United States out of it. For his efforts, however, Wilson was awarded the 1919 Nobel Peace Prize, the second U.S. President to receive it.

Wilson rode down Pennsylvania Avenue with his successor, Republican Warren Harding, but was too ill to stay for the inaugural. He and his wife retired to their Washington home, where they lived quietly until his death on February 3, 1924. By that time, Calvin Coolidge was President. He attended the small private funeral, but Mrs. Wilson barred Senator Lodge from doing so. Wilson is the only U.S. President buried in Washington, D.C.

Edith Wilson lived until 1961 and attended the inauguration of John F. Kennedy. She died on the day she was to dedicate the Woodrow Wilson Bridge, which crosses the Potomac River in the nation's capital.

Perhaps no President has been so qualified for the office—with the highest academic credits and staunch moral fiber—as Woodrow

Wilson is shown here leaving his Washington home to make his last public appearance on Armistice Day, November 11, 1923.

Wilson. He was a crusader and an idealist. He was a true reformer and a great leader. But he was human, too. He was impatient with those who disagreed with him and too convinced of his own appointed destiny. From his lofty perch, he sometimes could not see the rough and tough real world below. Wilson served his country well and although he played a major role in ending World War I, his greatest disappointment was that peace eluded him in his lifetime.

Names in the News in Wilson's Time

Charles Spencer (Charlie) Chaplin (1889–1977):

Internationally famous movie comedian, born in London. Motion picture debut (1914). Starred in such films as *A Dog's Life*, *The Kid*, *The Gold Rush*, *City Lights*, *The Great Dictator*.

David Lewelyn Wark (D.W.) Griffith (1875–1948):

Filmmaker, born in Kentucky. Credited with the birth of the modern cinema with such films as *The Birth of a Nation* (1915).

Charles Evans Hughes (1862–1948):

New York lawyer and governor, narrowly defeated by Wilson for President (1916). Secretary of state (1921–26); Chief Justice Supreme Court (1931–41).

Jeanette Rankin (1880–1973):

Born in Montana, pacifist and worker for women's rights. First woman in U.S. Congress (1917–19, 1941–43); only member of the House of Representatives to vote against U.S. entry into World War II after Pearl Harbor (1941).

Frank Lloyd Wright (1869–1959):

Often called America's greatest architect, born Wisconsin, noted for basic premise "form follows function." Architectural masterpiece, Imperial Hotel in Tokyo, survived 1923 earthquake—just as he said it would.

Some American Heroes of World War I

Colonel Douglas MacArthur (1880–1964):

Commander 42nd Rainbow Division in France. Promoted to general and became World War II hero, allied supreme commander southwest Pacific, general of the army (1944). Congressional Medal of Honor.

Colonel William "Billy" Mitchell (1879–1936):

Commander of 1,481 Allied aircraft in the war's greatest air effort, the assault on St. Mihiel (1917). Court-martialed for criticizing War and Navy Departments, convicted, resigned from U.S. Army (1926).

General John "Black Jack" Pershing (1860–1948):

Commander American Expeditionary Force; did not approve of slow trench warfare, preferred quick, fast-moving attacks. Chief of staff U.S. Army (1921–24).

Edward "Eddie" Rickenbacker (1890–1973):

Greatest American flying ace; credited with downing 22 German planes and 4 observation balloons. Congressional Medal of Honor.

Sergeant Alvin C. York (1887–1964):

Thirty-year-old sergeant from the state of Tennessee whose name became synonymous with bravery. In one attack, took 132 German prisoners and captured 35 machine guns. Called greatest achievement by any noncommissioned officer in a war. Awarded Congressional Medal of Honor. Movie honoring him (*Sergeant York*) won best actor Oscar for Gary Cooper in title role (1941).

Chapter Four

Harding and the Morality Panic

Warren G. Harding (1921-1923)

Looking back, America in the 1920s seemed a topsy-turvy land of flappers and jazz. Just out of a serious, devastating war, the country yearned for fun. Young men snapped on their bow ties and tipped their straw hats. Young women tapped their toes to the new sounds of Jelly Roll Morton and his band. Everybody wanted to get behind the wheel of a Model T Ford. News, comedy, and sports flowed out of home radio receivers. Babe Ruth—the Bambino—was a home run hero to small boys of seven and seventy. In some circles, mobster Al "Scarface" Capone was a hero, too. Movies flourished right along with the Ku Klux Klan, whose racist members hid behind white sheets. Artists were calling themselves the "lost generation" and nearly everyone was ignoring Prohibition.

The Eighteenth Amendment stopped the making and selling of alcohol in 1919. But Prohibition just seemed to make drinking more attractive. Bootleg (illegal) gin and whiskey were sold everywhere. It was made in backyard stills (distilleries) and smuggled in from other countries. Although people laughed at the law, which tended to reduce respect for all laws, many were paralyzed or killed from poisonous alcohol. In 1933, the Twenty-First Amendment repealed the Eighteenth, and liquor was once again legal in the United States.

Into this atmosphere of the 1920s came Warren G. Harding, who campaigned on the slogan "A return to normalcy." But what was normal in the 1920s? People were probably looking for the pleasant days of pre-World War I. But half the people now lived in cities. The automobile was making the nation smaller and the power of the United States was growing. Warren Harding got his chance in the White House, and that certainly was anything but normal. Sometimes called the worst failure of all U.S. Presidents, Harding headed an administration that was undoubtedly the most corrupt in U.S. history to that time. Big men and little had their hands in the public cash drawer, collecting illegally gotten money and stealing from the government under the leadership of a relaxed President who supervised others rather like a man walking around in a fog. This mess resulted in the most spectacular government corruption of all until that time—the Teapot Dome scandal (see pages 56–57). Harding himself was never accused of corruption and he died before his administration went down in disgrace. Congress at last had decided to do some investigating, bringing on, according to humorist Will Rogers, the "morality panic of 1924."

How did such a man with a rather undistinguished conservative record, who preferred a baseball park to a Senate chamber and a poker table to anything, who later said "I knew this job would be too much for me," ever get into the White House in the first place?

Apparently, it was easy. Perhaps part of it was that Warren Harding the campaigner looked like most people's idea of a President. He was tall and well built, with bushy black eyebrows and a fine head of white hair. His voice was rich and pleasant, his dress and manners impeccable. He was a decent and genuinely liked fellow. All that and some luck got him into the Oval Office.

He was born Warren Gamaliel Harding in Blooming Grove, Ohio, on November 2, 1865, the oldest of eight children. He would be the seventh, and so far last, President from Ohio. His mother didn't like his name. She wanted to call him Winfield, which his father didn't like. His mother gave in but called him Winnie anyway.

Young Warren grew up to be a good-natured, humble chap who wanted to please everybody. A biographer later wrote, "He hated to be forced to decide on matters that might antagonize people." It's easy to see that this trait could cause a problem if one is President. His father was a farmer who later became a doctor. He also bought a newspaper and set his six-year-old son to work. That started Harding's interest in journalism.

Florence Harding

Harding went to a high school called Ohio Central College where he mainly excelled in band and debating and graduated in 1882. He didn't like farm work or studying law or manual labor, all of which he tried. But in 1884, Harding and two friends bought a failing newspaper in Marion, Ohio, called the *Marion Star*. He didn't make it a howling success, but it didn't go bankrupt either. Then, in 1891 he met and married Florence Kling DeWolfe, a 31-year-old widow with a son. Harding was 26. Theirs was not a happy marriage. In fact, more than one of Harding's biographers claim not to have the slightest idea why they married. But they did, and the very ordinary newspaper did well due to Flossie and her fine business sense. She hired and fired and organized and administrated while her husband wrote editorials and played poker.

To the public, Warren Harding appeared to be the force behind the *Marion Star's* success. People liked him. He was friendly and a good speaker, and before long began to take an active part in Republican politics. Soon, he was urged to run for the state legislature, which he entered in 1898 and became its most popular member. At a rally the following year, he met Harry Daugherty, a shrewd politician. Daugherty took one look at Harding and said, "Gee, what a great-looking President he'd make!" Never mind, of course, whether he was qualified! In 1902, Daugherty helped

Harding to become lieutenant governor of Ohio, and in 1910, Harding lost a run for the governor's spot.

Harding's popularity got a boost in 1912 when he was chosen to nominate President Taft for reelection. Harding ran for the U.S. Senate two years later and, with Daugherty's support and expertise, made it to Washington.

Warren Harding loved the Senate. He didn't much like the work, but he adored the friendship and the prestige and the social life. His voting record was reliably Republican and reliably conservative. He distrusted labor and voted for whatever was good for business. He did share a record of sorts in the Senate, however. He had one of the poorest attendance records in the chamber, showing up to vote less than one-third of the time.

While he was a senator, Harding renewed an acquaintance with Nan Britton, some 30 years his junior. Thereafter, he often visited her in New York. Their child, Elizabeth Ann, was born in 1919. Harding, who had no other children, never saw his daughter in person but contributed to her support. The affair continued when Harding went into the White House. In 1917, Britton published *The President's Daughter*, a sensational book about their relationship. Warren Harding apparently had other extramarital relationships as well, although the moral attitudes of the time kept them pretty well out of the press.

The presidential election of 1920 was on the horizon, the first in which American women could vote. The country had had eight years of the Democrats and a world war. People were frustrated. The economy was suffering from postwar inflation. Leaders were divided over the League of Nations issue. Everything was topsy turvy. Nothing was as it used to be. Republicans were itching to get back to the White House. But how? And who?

Along came Warren Harding. He wasn't even thinking about the White House. He was just worried about getting back to his beloved Senate and his friends. So he started to make speeches. He was a fine speaker. "Why had we fought the war?" he asked. Europe was still in a mess. It was America that required attention. "America first!" cried Harding. Americans want a return to normalcy!

It certainly sounded good. The Republicans needed a safe candidate. They didn't want another split in the party. They needed someone who looked presidential, was conservative, didn't offend anyone, made everyone feel good, and, most of all, could be controlled by the party leaders.

The Republican National Convention opened in Chicago. The leading contenders were General Leonard Wood, former Army chief of staff, Illinois Governor Frank Lowden, and Senator Hiram Johnson of California. The convention deadlocked. That night the party leaders, bleary eyed and tired, met on the thirteenth floor of the Blackstone Hotel. This secret meeting, known as a caucus, inspired the political phrase "a smoke-filled room," meaning a place where shady political deals are made. The Republican chiefs looked around, and there was the darkest of dark horses, Warren Gamaliel Harding—perfect!

Well, not exactly. First, they had to find out if he had anything to hide. So, they asked him. Harding thought a few minutes and said no. Apparently, Nan Britton and his young daughter had slipped his mind. So had the long-standing rumor that Harding was part African American. Harding said no.

At two o'clock in the morning, the doors of the smoke-filled room opened on the presidency of Warren G. Harding. One of the leading party bosses, Senator Boies Penrose of Pennsylvania, had just one piece of advice to those who would get him elected. "Keep Warren at home," he said. "Don't let him make any speeches. If he goes out on tour, somebody's sure to ask him questions and Warren's just the sort of fool that will try to answer them."

Indeed, candidate Harding was kept at home during the campaign. The tactic apparently worked, or perhaps Warren

Harding was just what the doctor ordered for the United States in 1920. With Calvin Coolidge of Vermont as his running mate, Harding defeated Democrat James M. Cox, also of Ohio, by 404 electoral votes to 127. Harding got a whopping 60 percent of the popular vote!

A war-weary public got what it wanted—an amiable, presidential-looking, undemanding midwesterner who would not press for radical reforms or inter-

A contemporary American illustration shows women voting in a federal election for the first time, in 1920.

national involvement. As for the new President himself, he seemed a little baffled by the job. "I listen to one side and they seem right," he said, "and then I talk to the other side and they seem just as right, and here I am where I started."

Harding's administration did have some good points. He appointed three able men: Charles Evans Hughes as secretary of state, Andrew Mellon as secretary of the treasury, and Herbert Hoover as secretary of commerce. He named William Taft to the Supreme Court. He recommended a budget system for the federal government and revised wartime taxes. Since Congress had rejected the Treaty of Versailles, it fell to Harding formally to sign a treaty to end the war on July 2, 1921. Presidents usually sign such documents with a lot of pomp and circumstance. Not Harding. He was called off the golf course, signed the paper on his host's living room table, said "that's all," and walked back to the links. World War I was formally over. As for any foreign negotiations and treaties to be signed with other countries, Harding left that to Secretary Hughes. The secretary presided over a Washington conference in November 1921 that settled old differences among the

United States, Great Britain, Italy, France, and Japan. That was probably the highlight of the Harding administration.

There was little else to boast about. Harding brought to Washington a group of cronies who had helped him into the White House. He knew they weren't the most talented, the most experienced, or the most dedicated people. He might even have suspected that they weren't the most honest. But he owed them. He couldn't forget that. In addition, the President's method of supervision was not to supervise or scold anybody. The result, of course, was the notoriously corrupt Harding administration. Old friend and Attorney General Harry Daugherty didn't have time to prosecute anyone because he was too busy collecting graft on his own. Charles Forbes of the Veterans Bureau skimmed money from the sale of surplus war goods and fattened his personal bank account. He eventually went to prison, and his aide and accomplice, Charles Cramer, committed suicide. So did Daugherty's personal aide, Jess Smith. Numerous men, in large and small positions, were busy defrauding the government of money that found its way into their own pockets. Eventually, things got so bad that Congress had to do something. The resulting "morality panic of 1924" investigation uncovered more graft than anyone had dreamed of.

Interior Secretary Fall's acceptance of oil lease bribes, which were the basis of the Teapot Dome Scandal, was the subject of many political cartoons such as this one in the New York Tribune.

But the worst corruption surrounded Secretary of the Interior Albert B. Fall and the Teapot Dome scandal. Fall persuaded a trusting Harding to transfer federal oil reserves to his control. Then, Fall allowed private companies, such as Mammoth Oil and Pan-American Petroleum, secretly to "tap" two government oil deposits—the Teapot Dome reserve in Wyoming and Elk Hills in California! For this, Fall got hundreds of thousands of dollars in "personal loans." When discovered, Fall denied any wrongdoing and served ten months in prison.

Even the good-natured President began to feel the pressure. "I am not worried about my enemies," he said. "It is my friends that are keeping me awake nights." More than that must have been keeping him awake, however, for he did send Nan Britton on a European trip while he and the First Lady made a national tour.

Harding died on that tour, in San Francisco, on August 2, 1923, at the age of 58. His wife would not allow an autopsy so there was some uncertainty about the cause of death, although it was probably a blood clot in the brain. For a time there were rumors—unfounded—that he had committed suicide or that the First Lady had done him in. By his untimely death, however, he was spared the disgrace of his administration. As biographer Samuel Hopkins Adams wrote, "He died in time." The scandals lasted until 1927, at which time Britton published her book in which she pleaded for an estate to be given to the President's daughter. She lost. Mrs. Harding died less than two years later and is buried next to her husband in Marion, Ohio.

Warren Harding was probably a good guy. He was a poor President. But in an odd way, he symbolized the era. The United States was just emerging as a world power after its victory in World War I. And yet, the President had campaigned for "America first!" and the people responded, as though ignoring its new role and power. The legislature, with the people's approval, had outlawed the sale of alcohol with the Eighteenth Amendment. Yet, the ban was so grossly disobeyed that it was finally repealed in 1933. Everywhere in the country, the call rang out for a "return to normalcy," away from wickedness, back to the "old virtues that made America great." Yet, the men in

charge of running the government were anything but virtuous. Presidential looking Warren G. Harding, from small town America, seemed to personify that vision of old-time virtue. Yet, Harding was himself a drinker, a dedicated gambler, and was engaged in a long-time extramarital affair. As in the country itself during the so-called Roaring Twenties, virtue seemed to be a lot talked about and little practiced in the White House.

The Roaring Twenties was typified by dancers like these doing the Charleston.

Names in the News in Harding's Time

Willa Cather (1873–1947):

Virginia-born novelist who expressed dissatisfaction with the 1920s by reminding Americans of the past. Most noted for *O Pioneers!* (1913), *My Antonia* (1918), and *One of Ours*, a lesser novel for which she won the Pulitzer Prize for the best work of fiction in 1923.

James M. Cox (1870–1957):

Opposing presidential candidate to Harding in 1920. Ohio-born millionaire and state governor, chose Franklin D. Roosevelt as his running mate; defeated by the "back to normalcy" campaign.

Albert Bacon Fall (1861–1944):

U.S. senator from New Mexico; secretary of interior under Harding; secretly transferred government oil lands to private companies, disclosed as the Teapot Dome scandal.

Eugene O'Neill (1888–1953):

Regarded as America's foremost playwright. Born New York City, won Pulitzer Prize for drama (1920, 1922, 1928). Among most famous works: *Emperor Jones* (1921), *The Hairy Ape* (1922), *The Iceman Cometh* (1946).

Mary Pickford (1893–1979):

Beloved film actress called "America's Sweetheart"; born in Canada as Gladys Smith. Films include *The Poor Little Rich Girl* (1917) and *Tess of the Storm Country* (1922).

Billy (William Ashley) Sunday (1862–1935):

Iowa-born pro baseball player turned evangelist. A phenomenon of the 1920s were his soul-whipping sermons to large crowds, stirring them to a frenzied call for redemption.

Chapter Five

Keep Cool With Coolidge

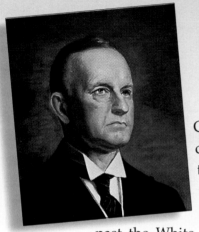

Calvin Coolidge (1923-1929)

*T*o believe all the stories about President Coolidge's lack of conversation, one would conclude that he said only about ten sentences throughout his entire life. Exaggerated or not, the stories are fun. Here are some of them. President Coolidge was walking with a senator past the White House. The senator said jokingly, "I wonder who lives there." Coolidge replied, "Nobody. They just come and go." He proposed to his wife with this romantic line: "I am going to be married to you." When kidded about his silence, he said, "I have noticed that nothing I never said did me any harm." He ended all speculation about seeking another term with these words: "I do not choose to run." When he left office, he advised his successor, Herbert Hoover, on how to get rid of long-winded visitors: "If you keep dead still, they will run down in three or four minutes. But if you ever cough or smile, they will start up all over again."

Silent Cal was a New Englander through and through. He was born John Calvin Coolidge in Plymouth Notch, Vermont, on July 4, 1872. His father, a farmer and storekeeper, was also John, so the boy was known as Cal or Calvin from birth and dropped his first name altogether in early adulthood. His mother, Victoria Moor Coolidge, was a frail woman who loved to watch sunsets and died of tuberculosis when her son was 12 years old. A few years later, Calvin lost his younger sister, Abbie, to appendicitis.

From the beginning, Calvin was quiet and shy, a loner with few friends. He said later that the hardest thing he ever had to do as a youngster was to walk through the kitchen door to greet someone. He grew into a slightly built man, about five feet nine, with red hair that turned sandy, fine features, a pointed nose, and a New England twang. He was never really in robust health and suffered from asthma and stomach upsets. Always an animal lover, as President he often walked around the White House with a kitten or small raccoon slung comfortably around his neck. He usually slept about 11 hours a day and liked to slick down his hair with petroleum jelly. He was as close with his money as his words. Even in the White House, he expected his proper change quickly—right down to the last nickel—if he sent an aide out to purchase something. He was also a rarity in politics—a philosopher and an honest man. Undetected much of the time was his clever wit, often turned upon himself. Of his friendly, outgoing wife-to-be, Grace Goodhue, who taught deaf children, he once said, "having taught the deaf to hear, Miss Goodhue might perhaps cause the mute to speak."

Calvin was a fair student but failed the entrance exams to Amherst College in Massachusetts, because he had a bad cold on the day he took them in 1890. After some prep school study, he was admitted to Amherst in 1891. Still only a fair student, he did gain a measure of self-confidence largely because he discovered that his dry wit could make people laugh. With the encouragement of a professor of philosophy, Charles E. Garman, who fostered the shy young man's belief in hard work and the welfare of others, Calvin graduated cum laude in 1895. Still a loner, he was now known as the campus wit.

Coolidge studied law at offices in Northampton, near Amherst, and was admitted to the bar in 1897. For the next few years, he practiced law, got involved with the lower ranks of Republican party politics, read and thought a lot, and was generally considered an "odd stick" even by his few friends.

Grace Coolidge

Then came love. One day in 1903, Grace Anna Goodhue, a graduate of the University of Vermont and a teacher at the Clarke Institute for the Deaf in Northampton, was watering plants on the school lawn. She gazed up at an open boardinghouse window nearby to see a slight young man shaving in front of a mirror. He was wearing long underwear and a hat. She laughed out loud. He looked down and fell in love. They were married in October 1905. The Coolidges would have two sons, John and Calvin, as well as a devoted marriage. Typically, however, Calvin did not discuss politics with her. She said in 1928 that she hadn't even known that he decided not to run again when he announced it to the press.

By the time their second child was born, Coolidge had served two terms as a Massachusetts state legislator. Silent Cal must have gotten his message across for he went from mayor of Northampton, to lieutenant governor, and finally to governor of Massachusetts, by a narrow margin, in 1918. It may seem strange that such a shy, reserved personality could propel himself into public office, but some of his shyness was countered by the fact that he was actually an ambitious man. He was not so much interested in politics itself, but he truly desired to help people. Besides, as he said later, he also wanted to please his father.

It was an incident as governor in 1919 that paved Silent Cal's way to the White House. A majority of the police in Boston, the state's largest city, walked off the job because the police commissioner would not recognize their union. Crime soared. Boston's mayor asked for state assistance. When Coolidge hesitated, the mayor called in the state troopers. Coolidge then sent in more state forces. He backed the police commissioner's decision not to rehire the strikers. When asked to reconsider, Coolidge said firmly with characteristic directness, "There is no right to strike against the public safety by anybody, anywhere, any time." Those words became a battle cry, and Coolidge was seen as standing firmly for law and order, especially by those who felt the strike was Communist-inspired.

A kind of revolution seemed to be taking place in America. The ordered world seemed so changed. Returning servicemen were embittered by the war they had just seen. They had come back to a country in which comfortable morals and social ideals were being challenged. The "Red Scare" was a hatred and deep fear of communism, which many citizens felt was responsible for what appeared to be dangerous changes in American values. The Red Scare represented, in a sense, a desire for conformity—for a return to what was perceived as "the good old days."

Unfortunately, it was also anti-Catholic, anti-immigrant, anti-Semitic, and anti anything that smacked of

Members of the Ku Klux Klan marching in Washington, D.C., in 1926.

being different. Not surprisingly, such hate organizations as the Ku Klux Klan were reborn in this atmosphere. What could be more conformist than burning a cross on the lawn of someone thought to "be different"?

Coolidge's newfound popularity did not get him the presidential nomination at the convention of 1920. He was, however, picked to become Warren Harding's running mate. As such, Silent Cal became vice president of the United States.

He wasn't much of a vice president, but then, few are. He said practically nothing at Cabinet meetings, which was no surprise, and he attended the required high level social functions under duress. He was so low keyed and so out of mainstream politics that the party wasn't even interested in nominating him for the top spot at the next convention.

Before they could discard him, however, fate stepped in. On August 2, 1923, President Harding died suddenly in San Francisco. Coolidge and his wife were visiting his father in Plymouth Notch. The farm had no phone. Three men arrived in the middle of the night. They woke Coolidge senior, who got his son and daughter-in-law out of bed. The elder Coolidge, who was a justice of the peace, gave the oath of office to his somewhat stunned but relatively calm son. After that, the new President went back to bed.

If President Coolidge was calm, so was his administration. He had inherited a party divided by friction and shamed by scandal. He was just the leader to quiet things down, which he did with skill and thoroughness. He turned over ordinary problems to his staff. Most important for his party, he restored its integrity. His policy was mainly watchful waiting to let things take their own course, such as the turmoil over the Harding administration scandals. He was slow to push for action. When Attorney General Daugherty would not resign for his part in the fraud, Coolidge did nothing. Only when Daugherty refused to produce his records and papers did the President ask for his resignation.

It might not have been good decisive leadership, but it seemed to be what the country wanted or needed—that return to normalcy. His party nominated him in the election of 1924. Soon after the nomination, young Calvin Coolidge, the second son, died of blood poisoning after stubbing his toe on the White House tennis court. Said the heartbroken President, "I do not know why such a price was exacted for occupying the White House."

With Charles G. Dawes as his running mate, Coolidge beat Democrat John W. Davis, 382 electoral votes to 136, and became President in his own right. His campaign managers cleverly used what could be regarded as a flaw—his lack of communication—to his advantage. The country was at peace and prosperous. Integrity and honesty were back in government. The man in the White House was calm and unruffled. Everything was okay, so "Keep cool with Coolidge." They did.

Coolidge believed that government should not interfere with business. Let it be. Good business, he felt, fostered prosperity. He kept the high tariffs that protected American business and relaxed regulations that might have curbed some questionable business practices. He did little to aid the farmers who were experiencing poor prices and overproduction. Coolidge believed they should fix their own problems. He vetoed farm relief bills as well as a bonus for war veterans. The latter was passed over his veto. Coolidge did not have a head for international affairs, but with the aid of excellent secretaries of state— Charles Evans Hughes and Frank B. Kellogg—he managed to improve relations with Mexico and went to Havana, Cuba, in 1928 for the Sixth Inter-American Conference. He ordered the U.S. Pacific fleet to aid Japan when that country was hit with a devastating earthquake and typhoon. He was against the Immigration Act of 1924 that banned Japanese from entering the United States. He did try to limit the growth of naval war power by calling for a conference of nations in 1927, but it was largely a failure.

America's prosperity in the 1920s is illustrated by this ad for a Studebaker, a popular car of the era.

Coolidge's reluctance to announce his intentions about running for reelection in 1928 elicited cartoons such as this one in the Chicago Tribune.

The country under Coolidge was basking in a period of "non-crisis," calm, restored integrity, and prosperity. But the prosperity was on thin ice, and Coolidge probably knew it. The stock market was sick and unsteady, warned some advisors, it was like a yo-yo, up and down. Financial experts were uneasy. Outstanding loans to investors were way too high. But despite the warnings, Coolidge felt it was not the federal government's responsibility to try to regulate the New York Stock Exchange. He believed that if he just kept up the public confidence, the market would steady itself.

At any rate, that was something for the next President to worry about. Calvin Coolidge chose to retire with his "I do not choose to run" statement. He never really said why, but some people thought that he was in ill health and just plain tired of the frustrations of government. Others thought that he saw the coming financial crash and depression and had not the energy or the will to undertake its solution.

Whatever the reasons, Silent Cal kept his word and stepped down with the inauguration of Herbert Hoover, who was unknowingly stepping into a national disaster. Coolidge and his wife retired to Northampton where he wrote his autobiography and magazine articles. With great sadness and some bewilderment, he watched his country collapse economically with the fall of the stock market in 1929 and the terrible depression that followed.

Coolidge died of a heart attack at his Massachusetts home on January 5, 1933. Characteristically, his will was one sentence long. He left everything to Grace. She died in 1957 and is buried beside her husband in Plymouth Notch, Vermont.

Editor and humorist H.L. Mencken once said that Coolidge's chief accomplishment in the White House was to "sleep more than any other President..." That may be so, but is perhaps a bit harsh. True enough, Cal Coolidge was not a forceful leader, or perhaps not a leader at all. He pretty much let things run themselves. But he gave the country something, too. He gave it back its belief in the integrity of the White House, which had been so damaged through the scandals of the previous administration. He was an honest man. That was good for the country, too.

Historians generally rank Calvin Coolidge as below average among influential Presidents. But, adds H.L. Mencken, "His failings are forgotten; the country remembers only...that he let it alone. Well there are worse epitaphs for a statesman." Indeed.

Names in the News in Coolidge's Time

Richard E. Byrd (1888–1957):

Annapolis graduate, with copilot Floyd Bennett, first to fly over North Pole (1926). Made rear admiral.

Clarence Darrow (1857–1938):

Spectacular defense lawyer from Ohio. In sensational trial (1925), defended teacher John Scopes who was charged with teaching evolution.

F. Scott Fitzgerald (1896–1940):

Minnesota-born novelist who wrote of the Roaring Twenties. Known for *This Side of Paradise* (1920) and *The Great Gatsby* (1925), which examined the thrill-happy times.

Greta Garbo (1905–1990):

Swedish-born U.S. film star, retired at age 36, rarely spoke in public thereafter. Pictured in magazine cartoon next to silent Coolidge, captioned "impossible interview."

Robert H. Goddard (1882–1945):

American rocket scientist; claimed in 1920 that a "rocket can reach the moon." First tested liquid-fueled rocket (1926), which rose 40 feet and crashed. Germans used his models to make rockets in World War II.

Charles A. Lindbergh (1902–1974):

"Lucky Lindy," aviator and American hero who gained fame with first nonstop solo flight across the Atlantic to Paris (1927) in his plane, the *Spirit of St. Louis.* Infant son kidnapped and murdered in 1932. Bruno Hauptmann executed for crime (1936).

Nicola Sacco (1891–1927) and Bartolomeo Vanzetti (1888–1927):

Political radicals charged with murder of shoe factory guard in Massachusetts during era of anti-immigrant U.S. climate. Convicted and executed despite appeals to Coolidge, widespread doubt of their guilt, and worldwide protests.

Cartoonist John T. McCutcheon in 1928 showed Charles Lindbergh elongated in order to accommodate all the awards he was given after his 1927 solo trans-Atlantic flight.

Chapter Six

Hoover: And the House Came Tumbling Down

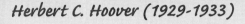
Herbert C. Hoover (1929-1933)

A Republican campaign promise in 1928 was "a chicken in every pot and a car in every garage." And why not? There was peace and prosperity in the land and honest government back in the White House. Everyone had been keeping cool with Cal. Why not continue with Herbert Clark Hoover?

The nation agreed. Unfortunately, instead of a chicken and a car, what Americans got was the Great Depression. It began in 1929 and lasted about ten years, affecting most of the industrialized world. It was the most severe and the longest depression ever experienced in the Western world. As many as 15 million Americans, perhaps 30 percent of the workforce, lost their jobs. They also lost their savings and their houses, in addition to their promised cars and chickens. By 1933, nearly half of all the banks in America had closed. Stocks were worthless. Life often seemed worthless, too. Many people left their families to wander the country looking for work—any kind of work. Others, in complete despair, committed suicide.

For all the good that Hoover did administering relief to wartorn countries after World War I, for all his fine service as Harding's secretary of commerce, he is remembered for, and criticized for, the Great Depression. Did Hoover cause the stock market crash that brought on the Depression? Of course not.

69

There had been dark warning signs for a long time. But did his policies do little to put the nation back on its feet and ease the suffering? Did he fail to grasp the enormity of the disaster? Was he too inflexible and rigid at a time when the country needed creative solutions? Many think so. For these reasons, the man often called the Great Humanitarian was scorned by his fellow citizens and voted out of office, his name forever linked to the worst ever economic period in American history.

Hoover, known as Bert to his friends, was born in West Branch, Iowa, on August 10, 1874. His father, Jesse Clark Hoover, was a blacksmith and salesman who died of heart trouble when Bert was six. His Canadian-born mother, Minthorn Huldah Hoover, attended the University of Iowa before teaching school. After her husband's death, she took in sewing and became a Quaker minister advocating women's rights. She died of pneumonia when Bert was nine.

With the death of their parents, the three Hoover children went to various relatives. Bert, the middle child, was given first to the care of his uncle, Allan Hoover, near West Branch and then to Dr. John Minthorn, an uncle who had saved the boy's life when he was about two years old. Thinking he had died of the croup, a severe respiratory disease, his parents had already placed a sheet over his head, but Uncle John arrived in time to save him. Now Bert went to live in Oregon with his stern Quaker uncle. Hoover's reserved, impersonal manner as an adult was encouraged by this devout family who also instilled in him the concept of serving others.

As a boy, Hoover was an average student and never graduated from high school. But in 1891, he took an entrance exam for the brand-new university established at Palo Alto, California. It was named for its founder, Senator Leland Stanford. Hoover was admitted at the age of 17, becoming the youngest student in the first class at Stanford. He graduated in 1895 with a degree in geology, having decided to become a mining engineer.

Hoover supported himself with odd jobs during his college years, including newsboy, clerk, and assistant with the U.S. Geological Survey. He grew into a tall and energetic young man with hazel eyes and a round face. He was self-assured, self-reliant, and somewhat cold. An efficient, hard worker, he was a poor speaker. At Stanford, Hoover met his wife-to-be, Lou Henry, daughter of a banker from Monterey, California, and the only female geology student at Stanford. They were married on February 10, 1899, after her graduation, and would have two sons, Herbert, Jr., and Allan. Lou Hoover, who died in 1944, was buried in California but later reburied beside her husband in West Branch, Iowa, after he died in 1964.

Lou Henry Hoover

From 1896 until 1914, Hoover was involved in mining work of one sort or another that took him around the globe. However, right after graduation, he was unable to find any mining work at all and ended up pushing ore carts at a gold mine. Finally, he was hired as an engineer for a project in Australia and then was transferred to China, with his wife, in 1899. During the Boxer Rebellion in China, a violent uprising against foreigners, he helped to defend the foreign community in Tientsin. Back in Australia in 1902 and then in Burma, he was able to amass a personal fortune of about four million dollars.

Hoover began to gain worldwide attention during World War I. From London, where his two sons were born, he headed the American Relief Committee, which aided stranded Americans. He was head of the Commission for the Relief of Belgium and director of the American Relief Administration. He distributed millions of tons of food, clothing, and supplies. Back in the United States as food administrator, 1917–1918, he got the

As head of the American Relief Committee, Herbert Hoover organized the
saving of food supplies to send to starving Europeans during World War I.

nation to "Hooverize," which meant to save food for the war
effort by going "meatless" and "wheatless" on certain days. He
was a skilled administrator, gaining praise for his work on the
War Trade Council, the Sugar Equalization Board, the European
Coal Council, and as adviser to President Woodrow Wilson at
the peace conference in Versailles. Economist John Maynard
Keynes later said of Hoover, "He was the only man who
emerged from the ordeal of the Paris peace conference with an
enhanced reputation." Up-and-coming politician Franklin
Delano Roosevelt had higher praise: "He is certainly a wonder,

and I wish we could make him President of the United States." Republican politicians just laughed and nominated Warren G. Harding in 1920.

One of the bright spots in Harding's administration was his appointment of Hoover as secretary of commerce, undoubtedly to repay Hoover's support during the campaign. No matter the reason, it was a fine choice. He was remarkably efficient at reorganizing the poorly run department. A firm believer in thrift and hard work, he instilled those concepts into his workers as well. He also saved the government a good deal of money by eliminating inefficiency. Among his achievements: he increased the information collected by the Census Bureau, expanded the Bureau of Standards to test more products, upgraded the nation's fish stocks through selective breeding, established the Aeronautics Board to develop commercial aviation, and got the steel industry to abandon the 12-hour workday in 1923. Hoover kept his job as commerce secretary into the Coolidge administration. One wonders why, however, since President Cal was to remark, "That man [Hoover] has offered me unsolicited advice for six years, all of it bad."

As head of the St. Lawrence Commission, he encouraged the building of the St. Lawrence Seaway (opened in 1959) and as head of the Colorado River Commission, he recommended construction of Boulder Dam. This engineering marvel on the Colorado River in Arizona, completed in 1935, still supplies electricity to Arizona, Nevada, and Southern California, and water to numerous cities. A popular tourist attraction, it was renamed Hoover Dam in 1947.

Silent Cal decided not to run in 1928. That left the door ajar for Hoover. He was nominated on the first ballot, with Senator Charles Curtis of Kansas as running mate. He wasn't everybody's choice in the party, but he did have the support of the Progressives who had backed Teddy Roosevelt and of women's groups. When he accepted the nomination, Hoover said these words, which would come back to haunt him in the not too distant future: "We in America today are nearer to the final triumph over poverty than ever before in the history of any land. The poorhouse is vanishing from among us.... We shall soon with the help of God be in sight of the day when poverty will be banished from this nation."

As anyone knows, you can't get in the White House without at least a little luck. Hoover's luck came in the form of his opponent, Democrat Alfred E. Smith, four-time governor of New York. Not that Smith was a poor choice, a poor candidate, or a poor politician. What he was, instead, was a Roman Catholic. Added to that, he

(left) A 1928 Republican banner proclaims the slate of Hoover and Curtis for President and vice president. (below) A Democratic party flyer in 1928 shows candidates Al Smith for President and Joe T. Robinson for vice president.

opposed Prohibition. Anti-Catholic sentiment in America had not calmed to the point where a Roman Catholic was going to be voted in, but Al Smith was the first to try. The persistent myth that "a Catholic can't win" was later put to rest with the election of John F. Kennedy in 1961. But this was 1928 and it wasn't going to happen. It didn't. Hoover was the winner, 444 electoral votes to 87. He was helped by southern voters, normally Democratic and Protestant at the time, who were reluctant to support Smith.

Inauguration Day, March 4, 1929, was cold, rainy, and dreary. A sign of things to come perhaps? But the new President was eager to begin his duties. Hoover was an energetic, hardworking President, up each morning at seven to do a little ball tossing out on the lawn before work. Lou Henry Hoover was an energetic First Lady as well and a brilliant woman writer, linguist, scientist, and scholar. Proficient in Latin, she helped her husband to translate a sixteenth-century encyclopedia of mining and metallurgy from Latin into English. She also did a good deal of entertaining during the Hoover administration. In 1930, the Hoovers gave a New Year's Day reception, inviting anyone who wished to come to the White House. Six thousand showed up! That was an awful lot of hands to shake. In 1931, they repeated the event. But by New Year's Day 1932, the Hoovers had had enough. They were "out of town" the following January 1. No President has revived the custom.

The thirty-first President of the United States had just seven months of the prosperity he praised in his inaugural speech. Then the bottom fell out and the house came tumbling down. Why? What happened?

The U.S. economy had been showing signs of trouble for some time. Many causes are given for the Great Depression. Weakness and imbalance in the economy had been hidden by the "good feeling" of the 1920s. Prior to this time, the federal government had traditionally taken little or no action when there was a downturn in business. It had relied on the market to right itself.

New York City's Wall Street, the nation's financial capital, was a hive of activity for the few days prior to the crash of October 29, 1929, as shown in this photo of October 25. The street was actually made of wooden boards to cover the construction of a subway line.

When too-easy credit and too much risk-taking in stocks brought down the house of cards, the government institutions were exposed as being unable to cope with the economic disaster. This brought on a nearly ten-year period of severe economic depression in the United States and Europe. When the bottom fell out of the U.S. economic market, Europe, which was greatly in debt to the United States after World War I, fell as well. Later, Franklin Roosevelt would make fundamental government reforms to ease the Depression, but it would not be fully over until World War II brought on vast production and a booming economy.

The beginning of Herbert Hoover's nightmare, and the nation's, took place on what is known as Black Thursday—October 24, 1929. Stock prices began a landslide on Wall Street. In a twinkling, wrote economist John Kenneth Galbraith, "22,894,650 shares changed hands, many of them at prices which shattered the dreams and the hopes of those who had owned them." But the next day the market rallied, shored up by investment bankers. President Hoover said, "The fundamental business of the country...is on a sound and prosperous basis." That Tuesday the bottom fell out of the economy and Republican prosperity. On October 29, 1929, the stock market crashed. It was, wrote Galbraith, "the most devastating day in the history of the New York stock market, and it may have been the most devastating day in the history of markets."

How bad was it? By spring of the following year, four million Americans were out of work. By 1933, the worst year of the Depression, about a quarter of the workforce was unemployed, and about a quarter of the banks had failed. Farm prices, already low, fell another 30 percent during 1930–31. To make matters worse, terrible dust storms plagued the Midwest. The storms literally blew away the topsoil on countless farms. An enormous number of homeless people began wandering the country, vividly portrayed in John Steinbeck's novel, and later the movie based on the book, *The Grapes of Wrath*.

Communism had an upsurge of popularity in the 1930s as factories shut down and businesses failed. Was democracy to blame? Men stood in breadlines waiting for a cup of soup.

This New York City soup kitchen is typical of many others organized throughout the country to help feed the jobless in the early 1930s.

Women worked in sweatshops in the cities for a dollar a week. So-called hoboes roamed the country, hitching rides on trains, asking for a handout. "Brother, can you spare a dime?" they said. The country was numb, paralyzed, without will or spirit. How could this happen to the promise of America?

At first, it appeared that Hoover and the administration did not understand the seriousness of what had occurred. The President assured the country that the worst would be over in 60 days. His first action was a tax cut. This was intended to encourage people to invest in business. But taxes were already low and little was accomplished. What Hoover wanted was for private industry to take the lead, but private industry was hurting, too. What Hoover would not do was what, ultimately, had to be done—the use of federal funds to create public works as an aid to recovery. It was against Hoover's so-called laissez-faire philosophy of individual freedom and little government intrusion into the country's economy. It was not that the President did not understand that the people were suffering. He knew it well, but he was unyielding in sticking to his conservative theory of government operation. He was convinced that government aid to the unemployed would lead to corruption and fraud. Voluntary cooperation was what he called for. He told the farmers "not to overplant." He told business to "regulate itself." "Prosperity cannot be restored," he said, "by raids upon the public treasury."

Hoover approved the Hawley-Smoot Tariff in the summer of 1930. It made things worse. He hoped the high tax would aid depressed American farmers by protecting them from foreign competition. Instead, the tariff enraged foreign nations and trade suffered. It was abandoned in 1934.

As things worsened, Hoover himself came to be a symbol of the Depression. The man who had once been hailed as a great humanitarian was jeered in public. His name was ridiculed everywhere. The newspapers that the homeless crawled under for cover were "Hoover blankets." A rabbit caught for food was a "Hoover hog." A collection of cardboard shacks where the homeless huddled were "Hoovervilles."

One of the most unfortunate incidents of the Depression was the "Bonus March" of 1932. World War I veterans, some 15,000 strong and jobless, pitched camp near the Capitol building in Washington, D.C. They had been awarded a bonus in 1924, but it was not due until 1945. The bonus marchers wanted it earlier. Congress, however, voted down the demand and many of the veterans left town. Still, thousands remained, a quiet and sad, ragtag group. Their makeshift hovels in the middle of the nation's capital city were a dreadful reminder of the condition of the country. The President ordered the army to clear out the camp. Some famous future war heroes obeyed the order— General Douglas MacArthur, Major Dwight D. Eisenhower, and Major George Patton. The camp was burned out. There were more than 100 injuries and an infant died from tear gas inhalation. In addition, film footage showed U.S. troops firing on U.S. civilians. This hurt Hoover's popularity even more.

During the Bonus March of 1932, unemployed war veterans fight Washington, D.C., police officers who were sent to tear down their tents.

Right or wrong, the impression was that of a heartless President. Hoover was widely criticized. He was not heartless, but he was rigid. He did support a number of public works and conservation programs, partly to provide jobs. More than 800 public buildings and major highways were built. He did approve the Reconstruction Finance Corporation. It loaned money to banks, farm agencies, and railroads. But that was business; handing out money to the unemployed was not.

Although all of Hoover's four years seem to have been focused on the Great Depression, other events did occur. "The Star-Spangled Banner," written by Francis Scott Key as the British bombarded Fort McHenry in Baltimore, in 1814, was adopted as the national anthem. Japan invaded Manchuria, in 1931. And Amelia Earhart became the first woman to fly solo across the Atlantic Ocean, in 1932. Adolf Hitler came to power in Germany, in 1933. That same year the Twentieth Amendment to the U.S. Constitution was adopted, changing Inauguration Day from March 4 to January 20. Called the "lame duck" amendment, it shortened the time that an outgoing President had to remain in office "doing nothing."

Surprisingly enough, as the election of 1932 neared, Hoover seemed optimistic. He believed that his reelection was crucial to the nation's recovery. At least he said so. The public disagreed. Hoover was defeated, 472 electoral votes to 59, by Democrat Franklin Delano Roosevelt, who said he had a plan to put the country back on its economic feet.

Hoover was out of the White House but not out of the public eye or public service. With his wife, he retired to Palo Alto, California, although in his later years he resided mostly in New York City. He was very critical of Roosevelt and his "New Deal" policies and campaigned against him in 1936. Hoover was strongly against U.S. involvement in World War II, as FDR was at first. Having met Adolf Hitler shortly before fighting broke out in Europe, Hoover thought the Nazi leader was

As coordinator of the Food Supply for World Famine, Hoover toured Europe in 1946 to determine the needs of ordinary people, suffering from the consequences of World War II. Here he walks through the rubble of Warsaw's "Old City" in Poland.

intelligent, although "partly insane."

After the Japanese attacked Pearl Harbor in December 1941, Hoover no longer opposed U.S. entry into the war. He served as chairman of relief for Poland, Belgium, and Finland. President Harry Truman appointed him as coordinator of the Food Supply for World Famine in 1946.

In retirement, Hoover is most remembered for the Hoover Commission, formally known as the Commission on Organization of the Executive Branch of the Government, 1947–49. About two-thirds of its many recommendations on streamlining government were adopted, such as combining department functions and tightening lines of authority from the President to the rest of the executive branch.

In the late twentieth century, it is not unusual for one or more ex-Presidents to be alive and well, but it was somewhat of a rarity in Hoover's time. Between 1933 when Coolidge died and 1953 when Truman left office, Hoover was the only living ex-President. He attended Republican conventions and other affairs and was treated like the grand old man of the Republican party, which of course he was. Shortly before his death, he endorsed Republican conservative Barry Goldwater for President. But he did not live long enough to see a relative make it to the White House. Hoover was a distant cousin to Richard M. Nixon.

Busy and active all his life, Herbert Hoover died in New York City, on October 20, 1964, after an operation for internal bleeding. He was 90 years old, having lived longer than any other President except John Adams, who died at the age of 91.

In the late 1940s, the magazine *Collier's Weekly* said of Hoover, "Like all Presidents, Mr. Hoover made his mistakes. But for years his political opponents unjustly held him responsible for the depression of the thirties. His distinguished career of public service was forgotten in a storm of insult and criticism." John Nance Garner, vice president during Roosevelt's first and second administrations, said, "If he had been President in 1921 or 1937, he might have ranked with the great Presidents."

Perhaps so. He was without doubt an able, efficient, dedicated administrator. In many ways, he was well equipped to sit in the Oval Office. But the fact remains that he was President in 1929, not in 1921 or 1937. His timing wasn't good, and history can be a harsh judge.

Names in the News in Hoover's Time

Louis Armstrong (1901–1971):

Called "Satchmo." Leading trumpeter in jazz history. Born New Orleans; gained fame in King Oliver band early 1920s; by early 1930s was bandleader, film star, outstanding jazz musician and personality.

Mildred "Babe" Didrikson (Zaharias) (1913–1956):

Born in Texas; called greatest woman athlete of modern times. Excelled in basketball, baseball, track. Won two Olympic events—javelin and 80-meter hurdles—in 1932. In golf, won U.S. (1946) and British (1947) amateur titles and U.S. Open (1948, 1950, 1954).

Amelia Earhart (1898–1937):

Born Kansas, American aviator, first woman to cross Atlantic Ocean in airplane (1928). Lost at sea on Pacific flight.

Huey Pierce Long (1893–1935):

Head of political dynasty in Louisiana, state governor (1928–1931). Flamboyant, czar-like ruler, appealed to the poor, maintained a personal army; was assassinated.

Alfred E. Smith (1873–1944):

New York-born state governor, known as the "Happy Warrior." Opposed Hoover in 1928 election; first Catholic to run for highest office.

Gertrude Stein (1874–1946):

American author who spent many years in France. Among her works: *Making of Americans* (1925), *Matisse, Picasso and Gertrude Stein* (1932), *The Autobiography of Alice B. Toklas* (1933).

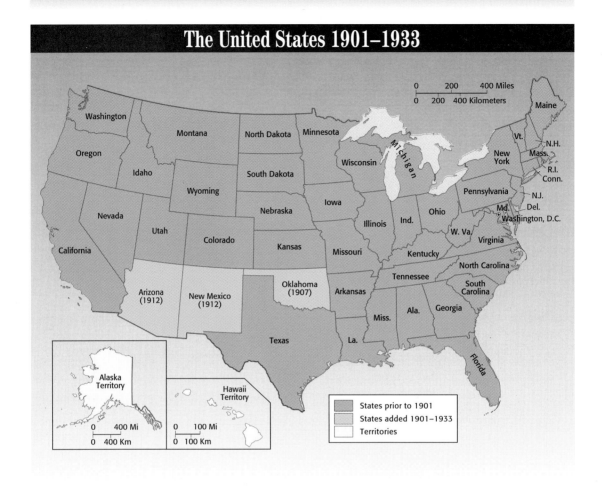

The United States 1901–1933

Washington
Montana
North Dakota
Minnesota
Oregon
Idaho
Wisconsin
Michigan
Maine
Vt.
N.H.
New York
Mass.
R.I.
Conn.
Wyoming
South Dakota
Iowa
Pennsylvania
N.J.
Nevada
Utah
Nebraska
Illinois
Ind.
Ohio
Md.
Del.
Washington, D.C.
California
Colorado
Kansas
Missouri
W. Va.
Virginia
Kentucky
North Carolina
Arizona (1912)
New Mexico (1912)
Oklahoma (1907)
Arkansas
Tennessee
South Carolina
Miss.
Ala.
Georgia
Texas
La.
Florida

0   200   400 Miles
0   200   400 Kilometers

Alaska Territory
0   400 Mi
0   400 Km

Hawaii Territory
0   100 Mi
0   100 Km

States prior to 1901
States added 1901–1933
Territories

During the early twentieth century, three territories were admitted as states in the "lower forty-eight," giving the United States its present configuration.

26. Theodore Roosevelt (1901–1909)

Republican party; age at inauguration, 42

Born: New York, New York, October 17, 1858

Died: Oyster Bay, New York, January 6, 1919

Education; occupation: Harvard; lawyer

Military service: Colonel, Rough Riders, Spanish-American War

Family: Alice H. Lee (married 1880), Edith Kermit Carow
   (married 1886); children: Alice Lee, Theodore, Kermit,
   Ethel, Archibald, Quentin

Important events during Roosevelt's terms:

   1903: Wright Brothers first flight at Kitty Hawk, North Carolina

   1904: Canal Zone acquired from Panama.

   1906: San Francisco earthquake

   1907: Oklahoma becomes 46th state.

27. William Howard Taft (1909–1913)

Republican party; age at inauguration, 51

Born: Cincinnati, Ohio, September 15, 1857

Died: Washington, D.C., March 8, 1930

Education; occupation: Yale; lawyer

Family: Helen Herron (married 1886); children: Robert, Helen, Charles

Important events during Taft's term:

   1909: North Pole discovered by Peary; first transcontinental
       airplane flight

   1912: New Mexico becomes 47th state.

   1913: Sixteenth Amendment, allowing income tax, ratified.

28. Woodrow Wilson (1913–1921)

Democratic party; age at inauguration, 57

Born: Staunton, Virginia, December 18, 1856

Died: Washington, D.C., February 3, 1924

Education; occupation: Princeton, University of Virginia Law School; educator

Family: Ellen Axson (married 1885), Edith Galt (married 1915);
    children: Margaret, Jessie, Eleanor

Important events during Wilson's terms:

1913: Seventeenth Amendment (Senate terms and makeup) ratified.

1914: Panama Canal opened; World War I begins in Europe.

1915: German submarine sinks *Lusitania*.

1917: U.S. buys Virgin Islands from Denmark; U.S. declares war on Germany.

1918: Wilson presents 14 Points for peace; armistice ends World War I.

1919: Eighteenth Amendment (Prohibition) ratified; Wilson suffers stroke;
    U.S. rejects Treaty of Versailles.

1920: League of Nations meets, U.S. absent; Nineteenth Amendment (vote for
    women) ratified; Wilson wins Nobel Peace Prize.

29. Warren G. Harding (1921–1923)

Republican party; age at inauguration, 55

Born: Blooming Grove, Ohio, November 2, 1865

Died: San Francisco, California, August 2, 1923

Education; occupation: Ohio Central; journalist

Family: Florence Kling DeWolfe (married 1860)

Important events during Harding's term:

1921: Bureau of the Budget and Veteran's Bureau created; Tomb
    of the Unknown Soldier dedicated.

1922: Washington Naval Conference to limit naval armaments;
    first woman senator appointed, Rebecca Felton of Georgia.

30. Calvin Coolidge (1923–1929)

Republican party; age at inauguration, 51
Born: Plymouth Notch, Vermont, July 4, 1872
Died: Northampton, Massachusetts, January 5, 1933
Education; occupation: Amherst; lawyer
Family: Grace Anna Goodhue (married 1905); children: John, Calvin
Important events during Coolidge's terms:

> 1924: Teapot Dome scandal prosecuted; Native Americans given citizenship.

> 1925: Tennessee prohibits teaching of evolution theory.

> 1927: First talking movie; Lindbergh flies the Atlantic.

32. Herbert Hoover (1929–1933)

Republican party; age at inauguration, 54
Born: West Branch, Iowa, August 10, 1874
Died: New York City, October 20, 1964
Education; occupation: Stanford; civil engineer
Family: Lou Henry (married 1899); children: Herbert, Allan
Important events during Hoover's term:

> 1929: Stock Market crash

> 1930: Boulder (Hoover) Dam construction begins.

> 1931: "The Star-Spangled Banner" named national anthem;
> Japan invades Manchuria.

> 1932: Amelia Earhart flies solo across Atlantic.

> 1933: Hitler gains power in Germany; Twentieth Amendment ratified.

Glossary

annexation The act of adding to something, such as adding the Hawaiian Islands to U.S. territory.

boycott To refuse to deal with an organization (or person or store) unless certain conditions are changed.

caucus A closed meeting of members of the same political party.

communism A dictatorial system in which a single party controls the government and the economy of a country, and private property is eliminated. The Communist system came into power in Russia as a result of the Russian Revolution of 1917. The word "red" originally became associated with communism because of Russia's Communist flag.

depression In economics, a period of low activity and rising levels of unemployment.

flapper A young woman of the World War I and following period who showed freedom from usual conventions of behavior.

franchise Special privilege or license granted to person or organization to sell specific goods or services in an area.

graft In politics, material gain by illicit means.

isolationism A country's policy of remaining apart from alliances or relations with other nations.

nationalism Devotion to one nation above all others.

neutrality Not taking either side, as in a war.

platform Statement of a party's policies or principles.

precincts In law enforcement, the divisions of a city for police control.

progressive In politics, relating to new ideas or opportunities and social improvement.

sweatshop Shop or factory employing workers in unsafe conditions for long hours at low wages.

tenement A dwelling house, usually denoting poor quality and occupied by people of low income.

ticket In politics, a list of candidates for election.

tycoon Businessperson of exceptional wealth and power.

Further Reading

Anthony, Carl S. *America's Most Influential First Ladies.* Oliver Press, 1992

Brightfield, Richard. *Roaring Twenties.* Bantam, 1993

Canadeo, Anne. *Warren G. Harding: Twenty-Ninth President of the United States.* Garrett, 1990

Carter, Alden R. *The Spanish American War: Imperial Ambitions.* Franklin Watts, 1992

Cohen, Daniel. *Prohibition: America Makes Alcohol Illegal.* Millbrook, 1995

Cook, Fred. *The Ku Klux Klan: America's Recurring Nightmare.* Silver Burdett Press, 1989

Davies, Nancy M. *The Stock Market Crash of Nineteen Twenty-nine.* Silver Burdett Press, 1995

Falkof, Lucille. *William H. Taft: Twenty-Seventh President of the United States.* Garret, 1990

Farris, John. *Dust Bowl.* Lucent Books, 1989

Feinberg, Barbara S. *American Political Scandals Past and Present.* Franklin Watts, 1992

Hansen, Ellen, ed. *Evolution on Trial.* Discovery Enterprises, 1994

Hilton, Suzanne. *The World of Young Herbert Hoover.* Walker & Co., 1987

Humble, Richard. *A World War Two Submarine.* P. Bedrick, 1991

McKay, David. *American Politics and Society.* Blackwell, 1993

Pancer, Nancy W. *Locks, Crocs, and Skeeters: The Story of the Panama Canal.* Greenwillow, 1996

Randolf, Sallie. *Woodrow Wilson.* Walker & Co., 1992

Ross, Stewart. *World War II,* "Causes and Consequences" series. Raintree Steck-Vaughn, 1995

Sharman, Margaret. *Nineteen Twenties,* "Take Ten Years" series. Raintree Steck-Vaughn, 1992

Smith, Betsy C. *Women Win the Vote.* Silver Burdett Press, 1989

Wheeler, Leslie and Peacock, Judith. *Events that Changed American History.* Raintree Steck-Vaughn, 1994

Wormser, Richard L. *Growing Up in the Great Depression.* Atheneum, 1994

Index

S